ROBIN LAING is a songwriter and interpreter of traditional Scottish songs. He has a particular interest in good whisky and has created a one-man show and a CD on the subject entitled *The Angels' Share*. The Edinburgh International Festival Fringe also saw him joining forces with Jim Malcolm to do a show called *Whisky, Women and Song*. As a result of this interest he has amassed a substantial collection of whisky songs and poems, many of which are in this new anthology.

The Whisky Muse combines two of Robin's passions - folk song and whisky - a powerful combination! When not exploring the purely cultural aspects of whisky, Robin is sometimes to be found on the Tasting Panel of The Scotch Malt Whisky Society. It's a difficult job, but someone has to do it!

Originally from Edinburgh, he now lives in rural Lanarkshire and has been a full-time musician since 1996. He tours extensively both in the UK and overseas, and has recorded four CDs – *Edinburgh Skyline* (1989), *Walking in Time* (1994), *The Angels' Share* (1997) and *Imaginary Lines* (1999) – all released by Greentrax.

BOB DEWAR was born at an early age in Edinburgh.
First published at 14, and in print every day since.
Political and social commentary for *The Scotsman*.
12 books for Oxford University Press.
Illustrates for The Scotch Malt Whisky Society, Leith.
Married to author Isla Dewar.
Two sons. Two Siamese cats.
No mention in the *Senchus Fer nAlban*.

D1354120

The Whisky Muse

Scotch Whisky in Poem and Song

Collected and introduced by
ROBIN LAING

Illustrated by
BOB DEWAR

Luath Press Limited

EDINBURGH

www.luath.co.uk

First Published 2002

The paper used in this book is acid-free, neutral-sized and recyclable.
It is made from low chlorine pulps produced in a low-energy, low
emission manner from renewable forests.

Printed and bound by
J. W. Arrowsmith Ltd., Bristol

Designed by Tom Bee, Edinburgh

Typeset in 10 point and 12 point Mrs Eaves by
S. Fairgrieve, Edinburgh

© Luath Press Ltd

Acknowledgements

Thanks to Raymond Vittesse for 'An Abacus o' Decay'; David Rorie Society for 'The Auld Doctor' by David Rorie; 'Hogmanay' and 'Ballade of Good Whisky' are from *Collected Poems* by Norman MacCaig published by Chatto and Windus - used by permission of the Random House Group Limited; Grian Music for 'The Best o' the Barley' by Brian McNeill, 'Bottle o' the Best' by Jack Foley and 'More Than Just a Dram' by Robin Laing; David Morrison for 'Brebster Ceilidh'; National Poetry Foundation for 'Christmas Cheer' by Patrick Taylor, first published in *A View From Suburbia*, National Poetry Foundation, 1992; Brown, Son and Ferguson, Ltd. for 'The Deluge' by W. D. Cocker, first published in *Poems, Scots and English*; Alan Reid for 'The Devil Uisge Beatha' and 'Shining Clear'; Moira Forsyth for 'A Dram'; Stumbletree Music for 'The Ghost wi' the Squeaky Wheel' by Tom Clelland; Carcanet Press Limited for 'Old Wife in High Spirits' and 'A Golden Wine in the Gaidhealtachd' by Hugh MacDiarmid; Flambard Press for 'Heart of the Run' and 'Maturation' by Gavin Smith; The Michael Bruce Memorial Trust for 'An Islay Malt' by Janette Hannah from their publication *A Mindin*, 1993; Jim Malcolm for 'Lochanside'; Strath Clague for 'The Morning After'; George Donald and Buff Hardie for 'Our Glens'; Famedram Publishing for 'The Politician' from Angus MacIntyre's *Ceilidh Collection*; Hazel E. S. Smith for 'Song: The Steeple Bar Perth' and 'Tak Aff Your Dram' by Sydney Goodsir Smith; Springthyme Music for 'Tak a Dram' by Ian Sinclair; Watt Nicol for 'Tall Tale'; Billy Stewart for 'Three Men Frae Overtoon'; EMI for 'Twelve and a Tanner a Bottle' by Will Fyffe and 'Just a Wee Deoch an Dorus' by R. F. Morrison and Whit Cunliffe; Bruce Leeming for 'Uisge Beatha'; Gerry Cambridge for 'The Water of Life'; James S. Adam for 'The Wedding at Cana'.

My thanks go first to Mike O'Connor for his work in transcribing tunes; also to Lizzie MacKenzie and the other staff at the Scottish Poetry Library; the Scotch Whisky Association; the Scotch Malt Whisky Society; and to Edith Ryan for baby-sitting when I had deadlines to meet.

CONTENTS

The De'il's Awa' Wi' th' Exciseman *taxation, smuggling and illicit stills – the whisky wars*

Ye'd Sook it Through a Clarty Cloot *men and women – the other whisky battleground*

Introduction

Sippin' whisky

In the 1970s, while I was as a student, I spent a summer working as a barman in the Arisaig Hotel. The cocktail bar, where I usually worked, had a reasonably impressive list of single malts available. This was a relatively new concept at the time and tourists would often ask me questions, like what was a single malt, which one was the best and which ones were local. In order to do my job properly, I felt obliged to do some research (on the job training).

I found out some interesting things. Firstly, whisky could be an enjoyable drink. This was a revelation to me. As a teenager, when I first tried whisky, I had not been impressed. But then I was given blended whisky, as people so often are, and I had no-one to explain it, to enthuse or champion the drink, no-one to tell me about its place in Scottish life and no-one to demistify the bits that needed demistified. In Arisaig I discovered what the Americans might call 'sippin' whisky', and I liked it.

Secondly, I found that the nearest thing to a local whisky on offer, Talisker, was also the best - at least the 100 proof version was. I would tell this to customers who asked, and found that for every one who enthusiastically agreed with me, there was another who screwed up their face. From this I learned that whisky preferences are entirely a matter of personal taste and that the customer is always right — well, nearly always. For a long time, my favourite whisky remained Talisker 100 proof. I still have a preference for the stronger tasting, island whiskies and my love of the high proof dram led me inevitably to the Scotch Malt Whisky Society, whose whiskies are all limited edition, by their very nature. In the company of such rare and interesting whiskies it is almost impossible to have a favourite.

I tend to favour old whiskies from sherry casks, but I also like the smokey, phenolic drams from Islay. The truth is that I like anything with a good character and a good nose, and there is a time and a place for different styles. The Islay whiskies might be fine for after dinner but for breakfast or a summer picnic you would choose something different.

You can get as much pleasure from smelling a good whisky as you can from drinking it. For that reason we need a revolution in the type of glasses used. Anything vaguely shaped like a tulip will do, whereas the straight beakers supplied in most pubs are purely for blends, and you would hardly waste time nosing those. I am aware that to many people in Scotland, someone who noses a whisky is strange, and anyone who sniffs an empty glass — in search of what the French call 'extrait secs' — is a pervert.

My interest in whiskies has steadily grown. I am not obsessive about it, but whenever you have an interest in something, some people will think of you as a snob or an anorak. I visit distilleries when I get the chance and I have been a member of the tasting panel (yes, we spit it out!) for the Scotch Malt Whisky Society for some years, so - OK, I might be a whisky geek, but the truth is that what fascinates me most is not the smell, or the taste, or even the feeling of floating euphoria that follows a couple of drams. It is the culture - the songs, poems and stories that surround our national drink - a world of imagination and creativity that testifies to the fact that whisky, for the Scots, is much more than just a dram.

I have had two or three major career changes since that summer in Arisaig. I am now a songwriter and musician with a love of traditional Scottish song.

Out of my interest in the songs and poems of whisky came my one-man show, 'The Angels' Share', in 1996, followed by the release of a CD of the same name in 1997. In recent years I have been taking the whisky songs to audiences throughout the UK and in other countries in Europe and North America. My collection of songs and poems continues to grow. When you look at a collection of material like this, it tells a story. I thought it was time to pass that story on.

Make mine a large one

One in 54 Scottish jobs depend on the whisky industry which produces over two million litres of Scotch a year. Two thirds of this is exported to 200 countries throughout the world. The biggest foreign markets are the USA, Spain and France - all of these now consuming more whisky than the UK. With an export income of over £2billion, it is one of the top 5 export earners in the UK and it benefits the Treasury by about £1billion a year.

In many ways the whisky industry is Scotland's only long-term surviving major industry. Shipbuilding, steel, coal and textiles have seen their day, tourism, financial services and Silicon Glen are on the way up, but whisky production has consistently been a hugely significant part of the Scottish economy for well over a hundred and fifty years. In the farthest corners of the globe, people who may know nothing about Scotland know about Scotch. And if it is Scotland's contribution to humanity, it's not a bad one at that!

History in a glass

The story of whisky making in Scotland goes way back into the mists of time. Someone, somewhere invented the process of distillation, but that was a very long time ago. Now, most people do it - the French make distillations based on grape (Brandy) and apple (Calvados), the Russians distil potato pulp, in the Caribbean they distil sugar cane, and in the USA corn. In the temperate climate of Scotland, barley grows well and we use it to make a kind of beer which we then distil into whisky.

There is a debate about who first made whisky – the Irish and the Scots both have a claim. It is generally thought that whisky, along with religion, came to Scotland from Ireland, but who knows? I have a suspicion that those commodities are more likely to travel in opposite directions. The Irish reckon that their Saint Patrick was responsible for giving them the secrets of distillation, but then we all know that Patrick was born in Dumbarton! Douglas Young argued that whisky was invented by Irish monks 'as an embrocation for sick mules'. This is an outrageous claim, later retracted. Monks were far too intelligent to sacrifice whisky in favour of mules. If it were poteen, it is just possible, though I doubt if it would do the mules any good. For all the extravagant claims about the medicinal power of whisky that you find in Scotland, I never heard anyone recommend it for external use and I never heard of it being prescribed for sick animals.

The first recorded reference to whisky in Scotland dates from 1494, when the exchequer rolls tell us that friar John Cor was making aquavitae. It seems likely that both for some time before 1494 and for some time after, people here and there, throughout Scotland, just quietly got on with the business of turning some of their barley into winter warmers.

The trouble started in the 17th century, when the government realised the potential income to be had from the taxation of whisky. It was bad enough when the Scottish government tried this (the Scots parliament first imposed a tax on spirits in 1644), but when the British government, as early as 1713, applied a malt tax to whisky makers, there was a great amount of resistance. Illicit whisky making became a cultural expression of the Scottish motto 'wha daur meddle wi' me?', and the entire 18th century was a battleground between the whisky makers and the hated excisemen or gaugers. There is little need to ask which side the ordinary people were on. This was an issue compared to which Thatcher's Poll Tax was a flash in the pan.

That the government eventually won this struggle is obvious, and perhaps a source of regret to many, but it is likely that the regulation of the whisky industry was a sine qua non for the development of real quality in the product. Making illegal whisky with a private still behind a waterfall or in a remote glen may have a romantic touch to it, but the whisky produced probably tasted good because it was forbidden fruit rather than because it was actually a great dram.

From that point on the whisky industry in Scotland went from strength to strength, steered by the vision, determination and entrepreneurial flair of a number of larger than life characters, often referred to as the 'whisky barons'. Legislation has sometimes helped and sometimes hindered the industry since those early days and some twists of history have had significant and sometimes strange effects on the development of Scotch.

For example, when the French vineyards were devastated by phyloxera vastatrix in the 1870s, depriving the British upper classes of their supplies of brandy, whisky was there to fill the gap. When the USA decided to go dry in 1920, the Scots, with their folk tradition of smuggling, took up the challenge of supplying the Americans with illicit booze. The immediate result was another whisky war, but the long term result was that the demand for Scotch was even greater when prohibition ended.

The success of the whisky industry has been remarkable, though not without difficult periods, for example the 1920s and 1980s when overproduction and other factors caused the closure of many distilleries.

Scotch on the rocks?

The biggest concern to the whisky companies in recent years is the realisation that young people are not turning to whisky, preferring 'light' drinks like white wine, mineral water, American beers and flavoured vodkas. If whisky is only being drunk by older males, sadly its days, like those of the older males, could be numbered. There is little evidence that the industry is reaching those younger consumers in the home market, despite a considerable effort to change the look of whisky marketing and advertising – older males in tweeds sitting in wood-panelled rooms with hunting trophies are out and wild-looking young women with barely-covered breasts are in. On the brighter side, if slightly ironically, women are drinking more whisky than previously. This is probably linked to the tremendous growth of interest in single malts in the last few years - women tend to go for quality rather than quantity.

In the 1970s single malts in bars were rare. Now they are fairly widespread. Most bars in Scotland will have a few malts, and there are an increasing number of bars with frighteningly impressive lists of single malts, in Scotland, England and many other countries. The biggest collection is currently thought to be in a hotel in Switzerland. The growth of interest in whisky has also rocketed. Around the world there are whisky festivals, Expos, auctions, Malt Whisky Societies, Clubs and Associations. The Scotch Malt Whisky Society now has 15,000 members in the UK and the Swiss branch developed a membership of 2,500 in the first five years. The number of publications (books and magazines) has multiplied, along with dedicated web sites. More recently it is the specialised end of the single malt market that is running ahead - unusual bottlings, special finishes, cask strength and single cask whiskies. For many people it has moved from being a drink to becoming a hobby.

Aye, but whose?

Less than 25% of Scotch whisky is produced by Scottish companies. This is not unusual - a similar position holds in Ireland. Globalisation and the power of the multi-nationals is a fact of modern life. There is no particular evidence that this reality is damaging the whisky industry. It is still the biggest whisky industry in the world (four times the size of its nearest competitor), it is not in decline (despite predictions), and most crucially it still has a Scottish image and identity. This means that the cultural expression of our sense of ownership of 'the national drink' will continue. Songs and poems about whisky are not just things of the past.

Uisge beatha!

Scotland is a land of mountains, glens, river valleys and rugged coastlines. Energy is inherent in a landscape of high places, running rivers and seas crashing on rocky shores. To add to that energy we have one of the most changeable weather systems in the world. That is the context in which whisky is made.

Malt whisky is made from malted barley. The barley is encouraged to germinate, by careful control of temperature and humidity. When the optimum amount of starch and sugars are reached - i.e. when the shooting seed is literally bursting with life - the germination is stopped by the application of heat. This is traditionally done by spreading the barley out on the perforated kiln floor with a peat fire underneath. The heat stops the germination and dries the barley, and the swirl of smoke through the barley gives it the reek of the peat which it absorbs, affecting the future taste. The dried barley is then ground into grist and fed into the mash-tun where millions of litres of boiling water are added. The mash is agitated to get maximum extraction of the starch and sugar. The resulting liquid wort is passed to a washback, where special, fast-acting yeast is added. A vigorous fermentation follows, leaving a wash (crude beer) of about 8% alcohol by volume. This beer is distilled twice in pot stills. This is done by boiling the liquid. Out of the violence of this process, the alcohol evaporates first and is condensed at the top of the still, cooled and eventually runs through the spirit safe, where the stillman judges the middle cut, for the best spirit is found in the heart of the run. The whole process, right from the beginning is one bursting with active, dynamic energy, power and movement - surely the reason it is called uisge beatha - the water of life. It is elemental and alchemistic.

Then, the water of life is imprisoned in a cask and made to lie down for many years in a quiet, dark place. It is this incredible combination of energy in the making and rest in the maturation that results in the phenomenon that is whisky - truly 'more than just a dram'.

The real McCoy

Pablo Neruda, in his memoirs, recalls drinking 'Mongolian whisky' - made from fermented camel's milk. Remembering the taste made shivers run up and down his spine - now there's a surprise! The Indians and the Japanese make whisky, the Norwegians make aquavit, Canadians make rye and the Americans make bourbon and Tennessee sour mash. Closer to home, the Irish make whiskey quite similar to ours. It's time to go over a few point of definition.

'Scotch' means distilled and matured in Scotland. It also tends to mean blended whisky, but that is by no means a rule. It is a word not frequently used in Scotland, other than on the label - when we say whisky, we always mean Scotch whisky.

'Whisky' means a spirit distilled from a mash of cereals. It must be matured in wooden casks for at least three years and it must not be sold at less than 40% abv.

'Blended' means a mixture of grain whiskies and malt whiskies. Generally, blended whiskies will contain between 10% and 40% malt. The de-luxe blends may have 50% and the cheapest blends may have as little as 5%. Blended whiskies are normally re-casked for 6 to 12 months after mixing to allow a marriage of the components. The bulk of whisky (86%) sold around the world is blended.

'Single Malt' is whisky made only from malted barley using the pot still method and is from one distillery. Single malt is nearly always a blending of different casks at different ages, but always from within the one distillery. The age stated on the bottle must be the youngest age of any of the components.

'Grain whisky' can be made from any kind of grain, not just malted barley. It is mostly made from maize and is produced in a patent still in a continuous distillation process. It is much cheaper to make than malt whisky and usually doesn't taste nearly as good. When the gap narrows it usually because of the poorness of the single malt rather than the quality of the grain whisky.

'Vatted malt' is a blending of different malts from different distilleries, i.e. it is a blend that has no grain whisky in it.

'Cask strength' tends to mean that it has not been diluted. All 'normal' whiskies sold at 40% or 43% abv are diluted at the blending or bottling stage. Cask strength can still be a mixture of whiskies and so is not necessarily 'single cask'.

'Single Cask' which means what it says - whisky bottled from one cask. This is the product sold by the Scotch Malt Whisky Society, for example, and it is undiluted, unmixed and not chill-filtered. This is the real McCoy!

A wee yin that's a'

It has always seemed strange to me that although the Scots have been drinking a great deal of whisky for hundreds of years, it is only in recent decades that single malt has found a market, and even now it is a small part of the market. It has at least filtered into the popular awareness. Single cask whisky on the other hand is still a very under-appreciated drink. The blends continue to dominate the market. Scots have always shown imagination and inventiveness in making a little go a long way. This is evident from the fact that many of our national dishes are peasant dishes making the most of cheap ingredients - haggis, skirlie, stovies etc. Blended whisky is a way of getting the most out of cheap grain whisky by cutting it carefully with some decent malt. There are many whisky drinkers in Scotland who cannot understand why anyone would pay double the price for a single malt with essentially the same alcoholic strength. Even some whisky connoisseurs of my acquaintance admit to choosing blended whisky for glugging as opposed to sipping!

The Protestant ethic and the spirit of capitalism

A more interesting aspect of the Scots and their collective attitude to whisky is their apparent ambivalence about their national drink. Scotland has always been a nation of extremes when it comes to booze - especially what the Americans call 'hard liquor'. On the one hand there are those that want to drink copious quantities of it endlessly, to the point of sickness and eventual death, who want to praise it in drunken odes, dab it behind their ears, have it on their breakfast cereal and swim in it for recreation. On the other hand there is the section of the population that pray every night for God to punish the evil people who over-indulge, who would like to see it banned for ever and erased from our historical records.

Religion is the cause of these extremes. For over 400 years Scotland has been under the powerful influence of a strict Protestant church. There is a thread running through the Scottish character that is somewhat dour, strict-living, God-fearing and Calvinistic. That part infects us all - we grow up with it - and that is the part that would always have difficulty with anything as pleasurable and hedonistic as whisky. The Irish don't have the same ambivalence about drinking whiskey, they have no guilt and just get on with the serious business of drinking it. The church does not torment drinkers in Ireland - it absolves them.

Maybe it is natural that people who can expect to have their indiscretions forgiven at the next confession are going to be more relaxed than people who think that all sins will be stored up and cast against them on the final day of judgement. In a rather strange way however, the Protestant work ethic and the values of Calvinism may have contributed to the great success of the whisky industry in Scotland. While the early Irish whiskey makers were drinking their product and only bothering to make more when the last lot was nearly finished, the Scots were developing theirs, improving the production process, doing business plans and market strategies and ploughing profits back into the business. In the Calvinist way of looking at the world, drinking whisky might lead to damnation, but if you can make a successful business enterprise out of the production of whisky (just another commodity), then salvation might be better secured. Thus religious disapproval has had an ironic, if not perverse, beneficial effect.

Haud yer nose an' doon it goes

The ambivalence of the Scots to their national drink has left some interesting traces. For example, there is the tremendous mythology that has grown up about the medicinal property of whisky, the half-hearted objections to punishing taxation, and the polarity of extreme views for and against the national drink with the Temperance camp on one side and the whisky garglers on the other. Whether one is a reaction to the other, and if so, which one reacts to which, is a matter for debate.

Whatever the reason, the Scots do have a particularly gung ho, macho approach to drinking - delighting in the idea of consuming vast quantities of alcohol, especially the cratur, our national drink. This is not a widespread phenomenon in Europe - indeed those very countries that have a more Catholic, relaxed approach to alcohol have very little evidence of problem social drinking. It is the cold, northern Protestant countries that do. Even here, only the Finns and possibly the Icelanders can match the Scots in their enthusiasm for strong drink. The Irish talk a good case, but actually their approach to alcohol is much more civilised than they like to pretend.

Blythe, boskie and borajo

The Scots language (and most of the material in this volume is in Scots) is rich in words for whisky; dram, drappie, barley bree, juice o' the barley, mountain dew, wee goldie, John Barleycorn, right guid-willie waught, wee sensation, blue, snifter, hooch, etc. and there are many words for the act of having a drink; swallie, skite, bender, etc., but the greatest number of words by far are for the state of inebriation and its various stages, stotious, stoatin, fu', fu' as a puggie, miraculous, roarin fu', blind drunk, pished, blootered, wellied, reekin, mortal, paralytic, legless, etc. Charles MacLean has made a study of the language and vocabulary of drunkenness in Scotland, asserting that each term can be placed on a continuum from tipsy to terminated and that each term quite carefully reflects a stage in the process of inebriation or a symptom of that stage, from blythe through boskie to borajo. Scots words for drunkenness, when examined closely, are about close and careful classification and description, much the same way that people like the Innuit, whose lives are so affected by snow have developed a more detailed and descriptive language for it than those of us who see it rarely.

The middle cut

The social and economic history of whisky is reflected in many of the songs and poems in this volume.

There are a lot of songs and poems and stories about whisky in Scotland. That is evidence of the importance of whisky in our history, identity and cultural and social life. This collection is by no means comprehensive. Every time I look into a song collection or visit the Scottish Poetry Library, I find more, and I intend to go on collecting them. There are also a number of exclusions that I have applied in my editorial approach to the book.

Firstly, it is not enough that there is a reference to whisky - the song or poem has to either be about whisky or to feature whisky to a significant extent. I have relaxed this rule on occasion, for example, in 'The Deluge', because of the quality of the piece and because whisky, if not central, is a powerful and wonderfully incongruous end-point. There are many songs that are about drink, for example, that are not specific enough to be included.

Secondly, this is a collection of Scottish material. There is an enormous body of Irish whiskey songs and poems. Equally, the Americans wax lyrical about it occasionally - there is a very interesting body of American Country songs about whiskey. Even the titles are fun – 'Whiskey Didn't Kill the Pain', 'I Won't be Sad Until the Whiskey's Gone', and my favourite 'Tonight the Malt is Single and so am I'. These songs and poems are for other people to put in other anthologies.

Thirdly, there is no Gaelic material. I have some in my collection, but as a non-Gaelic speaker, I am unable to assess the quality of them and I think in most cases, translations don't do justice to them. I regret the loss of Gaelic material, as whisky is such a Highland phenomenon, but for the reasons above and pressure of space, I have had to leave those out.

The keekin' gless

The material in this anthology is a cultural reflection of whisky, its history and the way the Scots feel about it. Quite apart from that there are some great songs and terrific poems.

The allocation of the songs and poems into eight groupings is inevitably subjective and possibly arbitrary. Different categories could easily be justified and many pieces could go in a number of the groups. Nonetheless, I think the groups I have chosen highlight the major recurring themes in the material. In particular they reflect our ambivalence. For every two pieces praising whisky (and there is a dominant theme of appreciation, gratitude and love), there is one carrying the sub-dominant message that whisky is bad and if you drink it bad things will happen to you. Each song or poem tells a story, but taken together, as a collection, more general themes emerge.

When we look into a glass of whisky we see ourselves. The picture is distorted and flowing, like a fairground mirror, but the reality is that we Scots do have quirky, peculiar and contradictory aspects to our nature. That only makes us more interesting, at least to ourselves, and, like the drunk man looking at the thistle, the whisky muse provides us with a valuable poetic insight.

More than just a Dram

THE ALCHEMY OF MAKING

With a process as magical and alchemistic as distilling whisky, it is inevitable that there will be songs and poems either about the process itself or using aspects of it as metaphor. Majestic pagoda roofs dot the landscape and the smells from malting, brewing and distilling waft around the hillsides. Trucks and tankers wearing delicious names and carrying unimaginable loads sweep gracefully round the curves of the A9. From every distillery, bonded warehouse and bottling plant the angels' share evaporates into the atmosphere. It is possible that the angels miss some of it, either accidentally or on purpose, and that these swirling vapours get caught up in the weather systems, eventually seeping out of the atmosphere into the creative soul of the Scots. We have it on the best authority, from Robert Burns himself, that his muse was enhanced by whisky and I have found myself inspired by it on occasion.

More than just a Dram

ROBIN LAING

Take clear water from the hill
and barley from the lowlands,
take a master craftsman's skill
and something harder to define,
like secrets in the shape of coppered still
or the slow, silent, magic work of time.

Whisky, you're the Devil in disguise,
at least to some that's the way it seems,
but you're more like an angel in my eyes,
catch the heady vapours as they rise
and turn them into dreams.

Bring home sherry casks from Spain,
Sanlucar de Barrameda,
and fill them up again
with the spirit of the land.
Then let the wood work to the spirit's gain
in a process no-one fully understands.

Whisky, you're, &c.

Now, the spirit starts out clear
but see the transformation
after many patient year
when at last the tale unfolds,
for the colours of the seasons will appear,
from palest yellow to the deepest gold.

Whisky, you're, &c.

When you hold it in your hand
it's the pulse of one small nation;
so much more than just a dram,
you can see it if you will -
the people and the weather and the land;
the past into the present is distilled.

Whisky, you're the Devil in disguise,
at least to some that's the way it seems,
but you're more like an angel in my eyes,
catch the heady vapours as they rise,
and turn them into peaceful, pleasant dreams.

Whisky has to be aged for at least three years in oak casks by law. Good malts are often matured much longer.

In the old days, we would import sherry casks from Spain and, after consuming the sherry of course, we would use the casks to mature Scotch whisky. This was found to give a mellow character to the flavour of the whisky and also gave it its distinctive gold colour. These days sherry butts are harder to get hold of and ex–bourbon casks are more common. Some distilleries (e.g. Macallan, Glenfarclas and Glendronach) still prefer the traditional use of sherry wood.

The choice of wood, and the length of maturation, have as much influence on the final taste as any other factor in the making of good whisky.

The 'cost' of this wonderful aspect of matured whisky is the spirit lost through evaporation – 'the angels' share'. It has been estimated that four million gallons are lost each year! No wonder angels play harps and sing up there on cloud nine. This song makes the point that whisky is more than just a drink to the Scots – it's our contribution to humanity!

John Barleycorn *(A Ballad)*

ROBERT BURNS / ROBIN LAING

There were three kings into the east,
Three kings both great and high;
And they hae sworn a solemn oath
John Barleycorn should die.

They took a plough and plough'd him doun,
Put clods upon his head;
And they hae sworn a solemn oath
John Barleycorn was dead.

But the cheerful Spring came kindly on,
And showers began to fall;
John Barleycorn got up again
And sore surprised them all.

The sultry suns of Summer came,
And he grew thick and strong;
His head weel arm'd wi' pointed spears,
That no one should him wrong.

The sober Autumn enter'd mild,
When he grew wan and pale;
His bending joints and drooping head
Show'd he began to fail.

His colour sicken'd more and more,
He faded into age;
And then his enemies began
To show their deadly rage.

They've ta'en a weapon, long and sharp,
And cut him by the knee;
Then tied him fast upon a cart,
Like a rogue for forgerie.

They laid him down upon his back,
And cudgell'd him full sore;
They hung him up before the storm,
And turn'd him o'er and o'er.

They filled up a darksome pit
With water to the brim;
And they heaved in John Barleycorn,
To let him sink or swim!

They laid him out upon the floor,
To work him farther woe;
And still, as signs of life appear'd,
They toss'd him to and fro.

They wasted o'er a scorching flame
The marrow of his bones;
But a miller used him worst of all,
For he crush'd him between two stones.

And they hae ta'en his very heart's blood,
And drank it round and round;
And still the more and more they drank,
Their joy did more abound.

John Barleycorn was a hero bold,
Of noble enterprise;
For if you do but taste his blood,
'Twill make your courage rise.

'Twill make a man forget his woe;
'Twill heighten all his joy:
'Twill make the widow's heart to sing,
'Though the tear were in her eye.

Then let us toast John Barleycorn,
Each man a glass in hand;
And may his great prosperity
Ne'er fail in old Scotland!

This very old song was worked over by Robert Burns but I found the tune in the bottom of a whisky glass. The personification of barley into John Barleycorn allows the song to describe the various stages of processing the barley in a wonderfully dramatic way.

Whisky is made from three very simple ingredients – water, barley and yeast.

The barley is encouraged to germinate and then, at just the appropriate moment, the germination is killed by the application of heat. Traditionally this is done in drying kilns over peat fires and peat has a very important influence on the taste of the whisky. The most heavily peated whiskies come from Islay, but all distilleries

(apart from Glengoyne) use some in the preparation of their malt.

This is an excellent version of John Barleycorn, though the song is much more popular in England, where it means beer, rather than whisky. This is because the English lost the second part of the recipe!

Address to the Barley Seed

ANONYMOUS

When the Lord first planted oot the earth wi' trees an' flo'ers an' weeds,
He scattered roon' Speyside a puckle barley seeds;
Thus was the birth o' Scotia's brew on that fair springtime morn,
For in the month that followed, John Barleycorn was born.

The threshin' plant had scarce made off, the golden grain was cairted,
Syne bags for siller were exchanged an' industry was started.
O barley seed, had ye but known the fate that lay before ye,
The very day in which ye breared ye'd ha'e telt the earth tae smo'er ye.

Regardless o' yer injured pride, yer golden grains sae gleamin',
They ran ye on conveyor belts that in a steep were teemin',
An' there ye lay for 'oors on end, sae soakin' an' sae sodden.
Syne they spread ye oot tae dry, trampled on an' trodden.

Frae there they took ye tae the kiln, ye thocht they'd only toast ye.
They held on coke an' peats until, ye thocht, 'My God, they'll roast me!'
They sent ye tae the millroom an' they hackit an' they cut ye.
Syne they sent ye aff again, in the Glory Hole they shut ye.

An' so ye cam' tae the day o' days when the mashman started mashin';
They pushed ye doon the hopper in tae the mashtun splashin';
They soaked ye in the bilin' bree an' drained the watter aff;
They sheeled ye doon the drag hole an' noo yer only draff.

O whit a come doon tae yer pride, wee golden barley seed,
Tae think ye'd land in sic a soss for the sake o' human greed.
Tae think that once yer golden grains were shimmerin' in the breeze
An' noo yer lyin' stinkin' like ony mouldy cheese.

But ye've ae consolation that canna fail tae cheer ye,
For noo there's millions love ye, aye, an' millions also fear ye.
Noo ye're in a bottle, in the world ye stand supreme -
The world wad gang doon on its knees tae ye O Mountain Cream.

They preach ye frae the pulpit, an' mony a woman's cursed ye,
Aye, an' mony a cheel when he threw the mash wad cherish ye and nurse ye.
Ye bring a sparkle tae the e'e, ye also bring a tear,
Ye've saved a life, ye've caused a death, ye inspire baith pluck an' fear.
In solace noo, wee barley seed, or is it barley bree?
I'd like tae say that ilka day my hand gangs oot for ye,
At seven o' clock each mornin', at five o'clock each nicht.
If I should fail tae find ye, I'd drap doon deid wi' fricht.

The authorship of this poem is not known, but judging by the language and the reference to 'dram times' in the last verse, it was clearly written by a distillery worker. In some distilleries workers were given drams straight from the still as well as decent matured stuff (sometimes referred to as 'whites and goldies' respectively).

Distillery Working Conditions
Past and Present

ANONYMOUS

There was a time in days gone by,
As some o' ye'll remember,
Fan a' the stills closed doon each year,
Frae 'boot April tae September.

Some boys war kept on for the moss,
But they war very few,
Near a' the rest jist got their books,
An' signed on at the B'roo.

Some anes they cudnae dae withoot,
The coopers - ane or two,
They war kept tae check the casks,
An' save the 'mountain dew'.

Aye, things hiv fairly changed since then,
Thank goodness! Bless ma soul!
They a' get wark the hale year roon',
An' nae langer need the dole.

Aye, things hiv fairly changed since then,
In lots o' different ways,
A worker then jist had tae scrape,
An' buy his workin' claes.

He noo gets jackets, dungarees,
Hats, gloves an' buits as well,
An' then there's a' the safety rules,
So that he'll nae hurt himsel'.

Boys at a distance get a hurl,
In the aul' days they'd tae bike,
An' them that cudnae raise the win',
They simply had tae hike.

A worker noo gets a' he needs,
There's vouchers for his lunch,
An' a' on tap o' that he gets
A bottle aince a month!

Ye'd think that noo he's gey weel aff,
An' cudnae look for mair,
But seen if things gang on like this,
He'll get an easy-chair!

Some boys watch dials, press a switch,
An' sometimes turn a knob,
Aul' hauns, retired, were born o'er seen,
For noo it's jist the job!

The ither wark can noo be deen,
A' mair or less wi' ease,
Changed days, I wight, it eesed tae be,
A' swite an' elba-grease!

Sax tae sax, that was the shift,
Men vrocht wi' a' their micht,
In winter-time some day-shift boys,
Hardly iver saw daylicht.

Trowin' the mash tun, rowin' in coal,
For four/five oors an' mair,
Whilst ithers chauved at luggin bags,
O barley up the stair.

Aye, that was wark, I'll guarantee,
That job it wasnae fun,
Gin they had humped the last anes up,
Each bag weyd near a ton!

Nae luxuries, nae motor cars,
Nae wireless or T. V.,
Twas jist a bare existance,
On a wage o' twa pounds, three!

Aye, times war hard, they slaved awa',
Wi' little compensation,
Except the daily dram or twa,
By wey o' consolation.

Of coorse, these war the official drams,
A' dished oot by the brewer,
But – there war extras tae be got,
O' that naething was surer!

An' aye in case a search was made,
Or someane blew the gaff,
They'd fill a bottle on the sly,
Then plank it 'mangst the draff.

The boys got up tae a' the tricks,
An' though it was gey risky,
They seen discovered weys an' means,
O' gettin' at the whisky!

Some chaps war canny, ither anes
Jist didna care a hoot,
But, even they war cautious
Fan the gauger was aboot!

The nicht-shift had a better chance,
Fan the bosses war asleep,
An' aye, in case they war disturbed,
Their mates a watch wad keep.

Some o' them had anither ploy,
For they tell me this was so,
Fan the real stuff wasnae tae be got,
They'd fa' oot on the joe.

The warehoose boys war jist as cute,
Fan the gauger wasnae lookin',
They'd dip a plumper in the cask,
An' draw't oot full an' drookin'.

'Twas jist too bad if they were copt,
They got it in the neck,
They'd nae tribunals in these days,
It simply meant the seck!

I got this poem from Alan Winchester, manager at Aberlour Distillery. The main themes are firstly, how much harder working life was in the old days, and secondly, how resourceful workers could be in getting their hands on the product. Every distillery has its tales of the inventive and imaginative ways workers devised to get their portion of the Angels' Share.

PRESS
FOR A
CUP OF
TEA AND
A NICE
BISCUIT

An Islay Malt

JANETTE HANNAH

I hold within my hand
The Isle
Within the glass.
The life and times
Of loved ones.
The morning dew.
The sea.
The sun.
The sand –
And then, through that,
The smoke from Donald's fire
Comes drifting through the years.
The trout that Susan's man caught.
The breath of deer, then back
To days unsure,
When Somerled did rule
The wild peat covered land.
All this within
The glass within
The hand.

If you are in the right frame of mind, a good whisky can evoke personal memories, musings and associations. It can also evoke the landscape and something of the essence of the place it came from. This is particularly true of some whiskies from Islay and the islands. Both history and geography in a glass!

Heart of the Run

GAVIN SMITH

If only love required
stark distillery skill,
a simple flick of flow
to catch the middle cut,
but I've too many
feints and foreshots
in the run
from my heart's still.

Maturation

GAVIN SMITH

As with most people
age improved it for a time.
Harsh, clear youth
complicated to manners.

On one particular day
it started to go downhill,
slightly at first
so barely a loved one noticed.
The oak's good work
became its liability.

The skilled distiller
caught the moment right,
started to bottle –
his memory filled
with the time before
slump and grey hair.

Minute by minute,
through Bourbon butts
and refilled Olorosos,
the angels, stealthy,
claimed their share.

*These two short poems by Gavin Smith use parts of the process of whisky making as metaphors –
they speak for themselves.*

A Whisky Kiss

ROBIN LAING

Down in the still's dark heat,
bound by copper plate,
our love was forged.

It started out with just a sip
but even then we knew
that somewhere else -
in rivet's grip,
a force-fed pressure,
pushing upwards, seeking space,
would determine that our essences
should mingle, merge,
combine and interlace.

Unimaginable energy at play,
seething, surging, bursting at the boil.
the cauldron of a witch;
the quest of alchemist;
the blow-out after drilling oil;
the surface of a sun a trillion miles away.

And from that first intensity
this special spirit flowed,
fed by fire and smoke;
a liquid love encased
in harvested and crafted wood;
tempered strength inside a stronger oak
to hold it in for decades, firm and fast.

'Nectar and ambrosia distilled'
the fateful words the Cyclops spoke,
(before his frightful arrogance was felled),
and that was only wine - but this!
The promise of a never-ending wish,
a pleasure first to last,
a loving, breathing, bonding whisky kiss.

A few more metaphors blended together to evoke a special relationship and the role that whisky played in its development.

Ardbeg

ROBIN LAING

I saw shafts of sun -
heard the flutter of wings;
a rainbow kissed dappled water.

The malt barn held only ladders
and history played in the shadows
but new wood and fresh mortar
held the promise that sings -
'The still runs again in Ardbeg!'

After long years of sleep behind briers,
colour returns and the heat
bubbles and re-energizes;
the phoenix finally rises
from ashes of peat
and pirouettes on a fine leg.

Ardbeg was the most peated of all whiskies and was therefore prized by those who like that kind of dram. Douglas McKay, past chairman of the Scotch Malt Whisky Society, would always end his tastings with an Ardbeg, but while he talked the audience through the preceding whiskies towards the glorious finale, Douglas, like a faithful lover, would only have Ardbeg in his glass from beginning to end.

The distillery was moth-balled for about ten years until it was bought by Glenmorangie in 1997.

I visited the distillery in June 1998 and wrote this poem, delighted that the sleeping beauty had been kissed by the handsome prince.

Rhymed Guide *To the Highland, Islay and Campbeltown malt whiskies of Scotland*

ANONYMOUS

Name we first the brands that rule in
Islay in the Western seas:
Bruichladdich, Lagavulin,
Bunnahabhain, and Laphroig.
Once I (lucky fellow!) fell in
With a man who had Port Ellen!
Though, indeed, as good as these
Is Bowmore or Caol Ila,
Celtic Witch and arch-beguiler,
Ardbeg, Malt Mill. And I shall
Surely drink more Lochindaal.

Last port seen by westering sail,
'Twixt the tempest and the Gael,
Campbeltown in long Kintyre
Mothers there a son of fire,
Deepest-voiced of all the choir.
Solemnly we name this Hector
Of the West, this giant's nectar:
Benmore, Scotia and Rieclachan,
Kinloch, Springside, Hazelburn,
Glenside, Springbank and Lochruan,
Lochhead. Finally, to spurn
Weaklings drunk and cowards sober,
Summon we great Dalintober.

Children of the Highland hills,
Products of the Highland stills,
Now's no hour to ponder faults,

Toy with test-tubes, sniff at malts,
Open-chested we must sing:
Away with care - the drink's the thing!
Fearing neither sir nor madam,
Praise we Dufftown and Glencadam.
Wanderer over hill and moor,
Weary, welcomes Edradour,
Purchasing new strength to loin
With Glendronach or Glengoyne,
Glenlochie, or ripe Strath Dee,
Cragganmore and Benachie.
Pious priest at mass or matin,
'Mid the murmur of his Latin,
Thinks of Mortlach or Tomatin,
Sinning so, but is there any
Sin in dreaming of Balvenie,
Brackla, Millburn or Glenfiddich,
Cardow, Banff or Teananich?
Sailor after months of sailing,
Fishing, yachting, cruising, whaling,
Hears the joyous cry of 'land oh!'
Thirsts at once for choice Knockando.
Let the magistracy glower,
Let the law put forth its power,
He will drink the good Inchgower,
Tamdhu, Parkmore, Aberlour,
And damnation to the finny
Tribes of ocean in Dalwhinnie, -

Drink until the stars go out.
Not for us such deep-sea bout.
Quiet tipplers in our class
Are content with Glenfarclas,
Nor does fancy with us soar
Far beyond sound Convalmore,
Oban, Coleburn or Dalmore,
With mayhap a straying wish
Towards Glen Elgin or Clyne Lish.
Hopeful nephew bound to see
Wealthy and repulsive aunt
(Shadows of a legacy)
Should equip him with Glen Grant,
He will find the interview
Smoother sailing on Knockdhu.
When debate grows over-heated,
Chairs thrown down and men unseated,
To restore both law and order
Bring in Dallas Dhu, Glen Cawdor,
Speyburn, Longmorn or Strathmill.
Quick the tempest will be still
And sweet reason reign again
With the flow of Daluaine.
If an angel unawares
Your domestic table shares,
You will not be wrong to give it
Tumblers of the real Glenlivet!
Serious poets, short of rhymes,
As we all may be betimes, -
For *ars longa*, *vita brevis* -
Woo the muse with good Ben Nevis,
Though the wench will come no less
For Glengarioch or Stromness,
Scapa or fine Highland Park,
Lighteners of Orcadian dark.
Men will talk most brilliant bosh
On a diet of Ferintosh,
Argue, with emphatic oaths,
Black is yellow on Glenrothes,
Prove that four and four make nine
If encouraged by Glenfyne,
And, in paradoxic fury,
Square the circle with Glenurie.
Converts have been made, they say,
To some quite grotesque belief
By Strath Isla and Glenspey
And Glenturret (made in Crieff).
Cunning preachers rope the sullen
Heathen folk in with Glendullan.
In melee or collieshangie
Glentauchers or Glenmorangie
Timid mortals will inspire
With a high heroic ire,
Though their sudden fits of wrath'll
Quickly pass before Blair Atholl.
Leaders of the hopeless charge,
Rallying for one assault more,
Should have come equipped with large
Flasks of Pulteney or of Aultmore,
Or at least another score
Liquors veterans will think good:
Isla, Ben Romach, Glen Mohr,
Balmenach, Glenburgie, Linkwood,
North Port, Angus-reared at Brechin,
Aberfeldy or Ballechin.
While the vanquished in the fray,
Fleeing to the nearest bar,
Counsel take with Auchenblae,
Comfort seek in Lochnagar,
And, when human courage fails,
Stronachie the foe assails.
Scholar, drinking with a lout,

Knocked his boon companion out,
Bawling egotistically, 'Shall an
Embecile enjoy Macallan?
Craigellachie or Imperial
Are designed for souls aetherial!'
Sad that academic rage
Should pollute my peaceful page;
Class and faction I abhor on
Towiemore or Ord-Glenoran;
Ragged hat and top-hat glossy
Meet as equals on Glenlossie,
Bury hatchets in a hurry
In Glenugie or Glenmoray,
Talisker or Milton-Duff
(Damned be he cries, 'Hold, enough!')
Rounding off at last the story
(Highland section) put we Finis
With Glen Albyn, Tobermory,
Glenglassauch and Benrinnes.

This poem is quoted in Aeneas MacDonald's book 'Whisky' (1930). He claims it was the doggerel of some Sassenach poetaster. It may, of course, have been from his own pen. Whether it is doggerel or not I shall leave to the reader to decide. It is of some interest as one of the most extensive distillery or whisky list poems, and there are a few. It also has a tantalisingly large number of distilleries that no longer exist. Look at the second section, for example, listing the Campbeltown distilleries. There are now only two left.

This is one of the sad chapters of the economic history of Scotch whisky. Brian Townsend's 'Scotch Missed' (1993) is a fascinating book on the subject. Distilleries, especially the traditional ones with the pagoda roofs over the drying kilns, once graced the landscape of Scotland in a very special way.

A Bottle o' the Best

IN PRAISE OF WHISKY

By far the most common sentiment expressed in the whisky literature is that of affection for what the Scots, quite justifiably, consider to be the finest drink in the world. For some of us, it sometimes seems that there is nothing in the whole sweep of life more important. Amongst all the writers of lyric panegyrics and macaronic cantos singing whisky's praises, admiring and listing its fine qualities and dreaming of huge amounts, inevitably there will be some who resort to miscalling the competition and saying unflattering things about beer, wine and brandy, and indeed blended whisky. There will also be dark comments directed at the unco guid – those who cast a disapproving eye in the direction of the serious lovers of the dram.

Scotch Drink

ROBERT BURNS (1759-1796)

Let other poets raise a fracas
Bout vines and wines, and drunken
  Bacchus,
And crabbit names and stories wrack us,
    And grate our lug:
I sing the juice Scotch bear can mak us,
    In glass or jug.

Oh thou, my Muse! Guid auld Scotch
  drink!
Whether thro wimplin worms thou jink,
Or, richly brown, ream owre the brink,
    In glorious faem,
Inspire me, till I lisp and wink,
    To sing thy name.

Let husky wheat the haughs adorn,
An oats set up their awnie horn,
An pease and beans at e'en or morn,
    Perfume the plain:
Leeze me on thee, John Barleycorn,
    Thou king o' grain.

On thee aft Scotland chows her cood,
In souple scones, the wale o' food!
Or tumblin' in the boiling flood
    Wi' kail and beef;
But when thou pours thy strong heart's
  blood,
    There thou shines chief.

Food fills the wame, and keeps us livin';
Tho' life's a gift no worth receivin',
When heavy-dragg'd wi pine and grievin';
    But oiled by thee,
The wheels o' life gae down-hill, scrievin',
    Wi' rattlin' glee.

Thou clear's the head o' doited Lear:
Thou cheers the heart o' drooping Care;
Thou strings the nerves o' Labour sair,
    At's weary toil:
Thou even brightens dark Despair
    Wi' gloomy smile.

Aft, clad in massy siller weed,
Wi' gentles thou erects thy head;
Yet humbly kind, in time o' need,
    The poor man's wine,
His wee drap parritch, or his bread,
    Thou kitchens fine.

Thou art the life o' public haunts;
But thee, what were our fairs and rants?
Ev'n godly meetings o' the saunts,
    By thee inspir'd,
When gaping they besiege the tents,
    Are doubly fir'd.

That merry night we get the corn in,
O sweetly then thou reams the horn in!
Or reekin' on a New-Year mornin'
    In cog or bicker,
And just a wee drap sp'ritual burn in,
    And gusty sucker!

When Vulcan gies his bellows breath,
An' ploughmen gather wi' their graith,
O rare to see thee fizz and freath
    I' the lugget caup!
Then Burnewin comes on like death
    At ev'ry chap.

Nae mercy, then, for airn or steel;
The brawnie, banie, ploghman chiel,
Brings hard owrehip, wi' sturdy wheel,
    The strong forehammer,
Till block and studdie ring and reel
    Wi' dinsome clamour.

When skirlin' weanies see the light,
Thou maks the gossips clatter bright
How fumblin' cuifs their dearies slight–
    Wae worth the name!
Nae howdie gets a social night,
    Or plack frae them.

When neibors anger at a plea,
And just as wud as wud can be,
How easy can the barley-bree
    Cement the quarrel!
It's aye the cheapest lawyer's fee
    To taste the barrel.

Alake! That e'er my muse has reason
To wyte her countrymen wi' treason;
But mony daily weet their weason
    Wi' liquors nice,
And hardly in a winter's season,
    E'er spier her price.

Wae worth that Brandy, burning trash!
Fell source o' mony a pain and brash!
Twins mony a poor, doylt, drucken hash,
    O' half his days;
And sends beside, auld Scotland's cash
    Tae her worst faes.

Ye Scots, wha wish auld Scotland well!
Ye chief, to you my tale I tell,
Poor plackless devils like mysel'
    It sets you ill,
Wi' bitter, dearthfu' wines to mell,
    Or foreign gill.

May gravels round his blather wrench,
And gout torment him, inch by inch,
Wha twists his gruntle wi' a glunch
    O' sour disdain,
Out-owre a glass o' whisky punch
    Wi' honest men!

Oh whisky! soul o' plays and pranks!
Accept a Bardie's gratefu' thanks!
When wanting thee, what tuneless cranks
    Are my poor verses!
Thou comes - they rattle i' their ranks,
    At ither's arses.

Thee, Ferintosh! O sadly lost!
Scotland lament frae coast to coast!
Now colic-grips and barkin' hoast
    May kill us a';
For loyal Forbes' charter'd boast
    Is ta'en awa'!

Thae curst horse-leeches o' th' Excise,
Wha mak the whisky stills their prize!
Haud up thy han', Deil! ance, twice, thrice!
    There, seize the blinkers!
And bake them up in brunstane pies
    For poor damn'd drinkers.

Fortune! If thou'll but gie me still
Hale breeks, a scone, and whisky gill,
And rowth o' rhyme to rave at will,
    Tak a' the rest,
An deal't aboot as thy blind skill
    Directs thee best.

This is the classic ode to whisky – Burns at his best in the Standard Habbie stanza. He praises barley ('thou king o' grain') and acknowledges that his inspiration as a writer comes from whisky ('accept a Bardie's gratefu' thanks'). He recognises the anti-depressant qualities of whisky ('even brightens dark Despair'), its role in social events from harvest to Hogmanay, and in promoting social harmony ('the cheapest lawyer's fee').

There is the famous reference to Ferintosh and that most delightful verse slagging off the Excisemen, his professional colleagues ('curst horse-leeches').

A Dram

MOIRA FORSYTH

She discovers
how the malt
sweet and fiery
stings the tongue
of the unpractised drinker
a taste unacquired
and yet familiar
the tang of something
old, forgotten,
perhaps from childhood-
woodsmoke and honey
and a faint, far-off scent
of some oblivion she may know
years and years from now
if she goes on like this
setting down the glass
her head filled with dreams
saying, yes, I will,
I will have another.

Ah Yes! Woodsmoke and honey!
Women tend to have sensitive and
appreciative noses and seem to
prefer quality to quantity in whisky
(if not in most things). Maybe that
is why they are a fast-growing part
of the malt whisky market.

Now that she has the taste, this
woman could go downhill quickly -
and end up on the tasting panel of
the Scotch Malt Whisky Society.
(Incidentally, almost all the
'back-room' staff of the SMWS
are young women. Tells you
something.)

A Bottle o' the Best

JACK FOLEY

Oh when yer turn o' work is done and ye've earned yer share o' fun
In the pub ye start tae sup, ye're clinkin', drinkin' by the tub,
Through yer pint pot ye're perusin' and ye're boozin' till ye're snoozin'
And ye're losin' a' yer senses through the drink.
Ah but when a' they folk sae prim are swiggin' swill up tae the brim
Nips o' gin and numbered Pimms wi' lumps o' sugar rubbed roon the rim
Let them drink it till they drop, for the sly, besotted Scot
Will be breakin' oot a bottle o' the best.

Aye, let them stick tae a' the rest, gie me a bottle o' the best
The amber bead I'll down wi' speed, it's no bad taste or waste - just greed.
And a whisky still I'll kill, I'll hae ma fill and if I spill a gill,
Ye know I will, I'll lick it aff the flair.
I'll no touch Teachers, Grants or Haig, gie me Bowmore or Laphroaig,
Glenfarclas in a glass, ye want tae throw the top away,
For there's nae need tae pretend that ye'll need the cork again
When ye're breakin' oot a bottle o' the best.

Noo the English like their ale warm and flat straight oot the pail.
They aye slitter wi' their bitter that would slaughter Jack the Ripper
And they sip their cider rough, sniff their snuff and huff and puff
And as if that was no' enough, they start tae sing.
Of when Jones's Ale was New, John Barleycorn's fine brew
Fathom the Bowl, The Barleymow, Bring Us a Barrel, just a few.
But their music's far surpassed by the tinkle in the glass
When ye're breakin' oot a bottle o' the best.

And the Irish in their Pride o' Erin think they can deride
Oor golden watter wi' their patter when they're a' oot on the batter
Sixteen hundred pints o' stout, a drinkin' bout without a doubt
And if they havenae got the gout, they start tae dance.
Tae Father O'Flynn and Larry O'Gaff, Biddy the Bowlwife, for a laugh
The Young May Moon, The Garry Owen, The Blackbird drives them daft
But their jigs have nae appeal tae the Scot who likes tae reel
When he's breakin' oot a bottle o' the best.

Aye, a bottle o' the best is what it says, it's no
    nae jest
Nae Mickey Finn, nae bathtub gin, nae
    rotgut wine that tastes like Vim
Have nae fear, it's no like beer, malt whisky's
    strong and bright and clear
Aye, and it's also bloody dear – but what the
    hell!
For it belts ye in the belly like a heavyweight
    Lochgelly
Then a glow begins tae flow, six in a row
    turns ye tae jelly
Then ye dream, perchance tae sleep as ye fa'
    doon in a heap
Ye've broken oot a bottle o' the best.

When I sing this excellent song, I sometimes apologise for the anti-English sentiment in verse 3. The anti-Irish sentiment in verse 4, on the other hand, is entirely acceptable as they are our competitors in the making of whisky. The brilliant internal rhyming in the song shows that we can do that better that them as well.

Jack's song celebrates the superiority of a good malt over any other kind of drink, including blended whisky, which in his opinion, and mine, is best kept in the kitchen.

I like the deliberate mis-quote from Hamlet in the second last line. If you are one of those people who think Shakespeare as dull as dish-water, then you wouldn't have noticed it in the first place.

Our Glens

Tune by GEORGE DONALD and words by W D (BUFF) HARDIE

I love Scotland's glens,
And whatever else we lose,
Please leave us our glens,
Our glorious glens.
Our mountains are grand –
Ben Lomond, Ben Nevis too.
You can have all these bens,
But leave us our glens.
Glenfiddich, Glenlivet, Glendronach, Glen Grant,
Can you do without them? If you must know I can't.
Put a drop in a glass of Glenspey or Glendrottar,
It's a perfectly bearable way to drink water.

I'd willingly lose
Our culture or most of it,
For instance that mess
Called 'Full Highland dress'.
With the whole ethnic bit,
With haggis and Hogmanay,
I'd gladly dispense,
But leave us our glens.
Glenfarclas, Glenlochy, Glengarioch, Glenfaul,
I once knew a man who had sampled them all,
Glenugie, Glenkinchie, Glenisla, – that's plenty;
He looked sixty-five but in fact he was twenty.

Take our Highland schottische,
Our marches, strathspeys and reels,
Take our old Scottish waltz,
But leave us our malts.
Remove, if you will,
Our ladies' conveniences
And our gentlemen's
But leave us our glens
Glenturret, Glen Scotia, and last week Glen Fyne
Was rare at Communion when they ran out of wine.
Glenglassaugh, Glenlossie, Glendullan, Glenmorangie,
I prefer them to Cointreau, which I find too orangie.

Oh! breathes there a Scot
Whose views on priorities,
When laid on the line,
Are different from mine?
Take our jobs, take our homes,
Take anything else you will -
Wife, family and friends -
But leave us our glens.

This song, from the creative genius of the comedy duo, 'Scotland the What?', reflects the fact that to some Scots there is absolutely nothing in the world more important than whisky. The classic rhyming of Glenmorangie with orangie is not only funny in itself, but also gives a guide to all those thousands of people who insist on mis-pronouncing the name.

The Water of Life

For a 70th birthday

GERRY CAMBRIDGE

Seven decades back, from his mother's womb,
And more canty and brave than most children are,
Came a child to the world's amazing room;
Even the doctor said he'd go far,
For though small and plump and round and red,
Bum skelped, *Whaur's the Glen Grant?* Tam said.

It wasny worth comin aw this way
Nine lang months frae wherever I came,
Withoot a dram tae stert the day;
A dram, a dram, Glen Grant its name!
The doctor trembled and the nurse fled;
Glen Grant's the best cure for your fears, Tam said.

Older, he sat in his chair, as on a throne
With the verses of Omar, under the lamplight,
Rain lashing the panes as the wind made moan
Out in the wordless rage of the night;
The mind ranged time and the hours sped;
Glen Grant and a book is the best, Tam said.

On a frosty night he and wee Shug sat,
Wee Shug in fifteen coats, five pairs
Of trousers, a dozen of socks, and a woollen hat,
And shivering in those shocking airs,
Tam in his shirt-sleeves, beaming and red;
You're no drinkin enough Glen Grant, Tam said.

One night, like a field after battle, the room
Had dozens of drunken groaners strewn about;
Yet there remained one glimmer in the gloom -
A whisky glass! without a doubt,
And one still-capable arm and swaying head;
The nicht fer Glen Grant is young, Tam said.

On the night of the blizzard when the roof blew away
And the snow swirled in from the Arctic air
And on sideboard and TV and table thick-lay,
As wee Shug gawped, who sat as ever in the big armchair?
Glass in hand, as the snowflakes melted, kissing his head;
Summer's cam early this year, Tam said.

'Who's this Glen Grant?' asked one, not knowing;
Glen Grant was here afore the world was made,
He sat in the void alane gold-glowin,
Awaiting a world in which tae ply his trade;
Genius and gowden king and fool, he drives oot dread,
And opens the gates tae heaven, Tam said.

'Friend,' stormed a preacher he met in the street,
'You're doomed; merciful God will roast you in hell,
You'll be burnt to cinders from head to feet,
Your giblets and brains will melt, and well -
Will you beg for mercy before you're dead?'
Glen Grant, Glen Grant, Glen Grant, Tam said.

On the last great day when the Lord
In his mercy decided to rouse us all
From our long sleep for our last reward,
The fat, the short, the thin, the tall,
One didn't stir from his earthy bed;
I anely get up fer Glen Grant, Tam said.

When the good Lord came to raise Tam up,
Tam broke out a bottle he forgot he had;
He and the Lord each sampled a sup
Or twenty; and the Lord grew loud and the Lord grew glad,
As they propped each other up, head to head;
Noo d'ye believe in Glen Grant? Tam said.

Distilleries were set up in Paradise then,
And the shining choirs of angels sang
For that gift from the old world of women and men,
And togaed and laurel-crowned as the glasses rang
As even the Lord turned to whisky instead,
Noo this is - hic! - heaven, Tam said.

So tonight among good food outspread
Raise a glass, and raise a glass.
For new things growing green as grass,
For all things that in time must pass -
Except Glen Grant, Tam said.

Tam is clearly one of those characters for whom whisky is of fundamental importance – perhaps slightly unusual for one of that breed in having rigid brand loyalty. Religious tensions are never far away in whisky material. I just love the ones where whisky wins, but what else could have the power to see God converted by the sinner.

Whisky Johnny

TRADITIONAL

Oh whisky is the life of man,
Whisky Johnny!
Whisky from an old tin can,
Whisky for me Johnny!

Whisky here, whisky there,
Oooh! Whisky almost everywhere,

Whisky up and whisky down,
Oooh! Whisky all around the town.

I'll drink it hot, I'll drink it cold,
I'll drink it new, I'll drink it old.

Whisky made me sell my coat,
Whisky's what keeps me afloat.

Whisky fills a man with care,
Whisky makes a man a bear.

Whisky gave me many a sigh,
But I'll swig whisky till I die.

Whisky made me mammy cry,
Whisky closed me stabbud eye.

Whisky killed me poor ol' Dad,
Whisky druv me mother mad.

Whisky made me pawn me cloes,
Whisky gave me this red nose.

Whisky made me shun the booze,
Put me in the calaboose.

If I can't have whisky, then I'll have rum,
That's the stuff to make good fun.

Whisky killed me sister Sue,
Whisky killed me brother too.

My wife and I can never agree,
She puts whisky in her tea.

Some likes whisky, some likes beer,
I wish I had a barrel here.

Oh, the mate likes whisky an' the skipper
    likes rum,
The sailors like both but we can't git none.

Oh, a tot of whisky for each man,
An' a bloody big bottle for the shantyman.

If whisky was a river an' I could swim,
I'd say here goes an' I'd dive right in.

If whisky was a river an' I was a duck,
I'd dive to the bottom and suck it all up.

I wisht I knew where whisky grew,
I'd eat all the leaves an' the branches too.

Oh, whisky straight an' whisky strong,
Gimme some whisky an' I'll sing ye a song.

Here comes the cook with the whisky-can,
A glass o' grog for every man.

Whisky made me scratch my toes,
Whisky makes me fight my foes.

Whisky stole me brains away,
The bosun shouts, so I'll belay.

This is a sea shanty. Whenever you get an all-male environment, like in the old sailing ships or in the 'ferm toun' bothies of the North East of Scotland, you find songs of longing for the things they fantasise about – drink, women etc.

Usually there is a strong element of male boasting or bravado in the songs, and coarse humour – ways of disguising their wishful thinking. These elements are certainly not missing from this song.

Uisge Beatha

'From the heath covered mountains of Scotia I come'

BRUCE LEEMING

Thus Glen Grant's ancient claim,
But many more can say the same:
Auchentoshan, Knockando,
Lochnagar and Aultmore too,
Tullibardine and Tormore,
Malts, Glenlivets by the score.
Glendronach and Aberlour,
Balvenie, Tomintoul, Inchgower,
Milton Duff and Fettercairn
From the rich plains east of Nairn:
These I drink with great delight,
Their amber smiles a cheering sight.

Then, from the misty Western Isles,
Dark with peat and Gaelic wiles:
Talisker, Jura and Ardbeg,
Bunnahabhain, Laphroaig,
Bruichladdich and Bowmore,
Lagavulin, heavy with lore;
These are my friends when days are fraught,
Their comfort real, if humbly sought.
For happier times comes Scapa rare
And Highland Park from Orkney bare;
From gentle Spey Glenfiddich, Tamdhu,
Macallan fine, Longmorn, Cardhu.

So many more, whatever you mood:
Glenfarclas, Rosebank or Linkwood,
Glengoyne, Glenturret or Glen Mhor,
Glendullan, Mortlach and Dalmore,
Tomatin, Dufftown, perhaps Caol Ila,
Glendeveron, Bladnoch or Strathisla;
There's Glenmorangie and Springbank,
Old Pulteney of undoubted rank,
Glen Moray, Balblair and Clynelish,
Glenkinchie, Blair Athol, if you wish:
The choice is wide, no matter your taste,
But never a drop that you should waste.

Old Uisge Beatha, my friend through the
    years,
In laughing fun and bitter tears,
I thank you for your faithfulness,
In easy days or desperate stress;
On the best of terms let us remain.
I'm sure that there will be no strain,
But there are cases, many an instance,
Where friendship's helped by keeping a
    distance:
We should sometimes show good sense
And mix with others less intense,
So when we come to renew our bond
Each of the other will be more fond!

This poem, though it has an impressive roll-call of malts, gives a bit of cautious advice on drinking whisky – keep it for special occasions. As far as the really good stuff goes, who could disagree? So keep it for days when you want to celebrate still being alive.

The Glass o' Whisky

GEORGE BRUCE (1825–?)

Here, tak' a glass! - Na faith! - no ane!
Say *sax*, an' syne I may begin
To mak' an honest drucken din,
　　Wi' sensless gab -
For less, I'm sure, would be a sin -
　　Here's to ye, Rab!

A'e glass is hardly worth my fash, -
Jist birls awa' your guid hard cash;
Then tak' advice, an' no' be rash
　　To play sic plisky.
It is the *a'e* glass plays the hash
　　In drinkin' whisky!

Ne'er touch it, man! No' ane nor twa,
But clash the glass against the wa',
And say, 'Gude faith! You're gaun awa'
　　To tak' a walk
Doon by the burn - shanks-naigs to ca' ' -
　　Their drink to balk!

Or gin ye want to ha'e a dram -
Say sax, at least, an' no' a sham,
When wi' a kindred spirit, Tam!
　　But no' owre often;
And dinna touch the single dram -
　　The tippler's coffin!

Jist see him in the mornin' jink
Into the public-hoose for a drink,
Syne oot again as fast as wink -
　　His *a'e* glass doon!
He's neither time to speak or think,
　　The tipplin' loon!

Or see the maudlin' cuif at nicht -
If summer, then in broad daylicht -
Sit guzzlin' wi' ilk' donnart wicht,
　　For love o' drink,
Syne stagger hame in shamefu' plicht,
　　As fou's a Tink!

And this a' comes o' drinkin' *ane*;
Guid youth tak' tent, an' ne'er begin,
But frae strong drink awa' you rin,
　　For it's your fae -
It isna for the paltry sin,
　　But for the wae!

This poem also gives advice on how to approach drinking whisky – never have only one!

On Guid Scots Whisky

GEORGE BRUCE (c1800 – ?)

'A wee soup drink does unco weel,
To haud the heart abune;
It's guid as lang's a cannie Chiel,
Can stand stieve in his shoon'. — Fergusson.

O, Whisky! muckle's on ye said,
Sair on yer back abuse is laid;
Nae doubt ye're a mischievous jade,
    Whan frien's, owre free,
Hae been wi' ye, a fell sair head
    Ye often gie.

This looks, I think, a wee ungratefu',
A character by a' thought hatefu';
But to blame rashly I'd be laithfu',
    Or ill names gie ye;
For mony a time I've ta'en the gait, fu'
    Cheerfully wi' ye.

Tho', as I daunder'd hame at e'en,
I things hae double sometimes seen;
But ither times I've brighter been,
    An seen things clearer;
By ye inspir'd, my vision keen,
    Made a' things cheer'er.

Nae doubt I've seen thy vot'ries tum'le,
Through dubs an' holes, wi' unco
    rum'le;
Yet, tho' ye gar'd them stot an' stum'le,
    Wi' fearfu' motion,
They ne'er at ye did girn or grum'le,
    Ye soothing potion!

Ye sometimes, too, displace the Graces,
Mak' noses blue, an' pluiky faces;
On droothie mortals leave sic traces
    O yer sad wark,
As gars the guid, in haly places,
    Sair at ye bark.

Ye aft do play the deil at hame,
An' bring grim Poortith, sullen dame,
Wi' a' her train o' ill an' shame,
    On bairns sae bonny;
Whan sic fa's out, I sair ye blame,
    Wi' curses mony.

Some too ye vex wi' drunken wives,
Whar sic plagues are, hame seldom
    thrives;
Folks drag uncomfortable lives,
    Wi' wardless helpmate;
Whan Whisky wi' sic jades connives,
    She should be skelpit.

Some ither pranks I here cou'd tell,
But brawly ken I wish ye well,
An' dinna like owre lang to dwell
    On ilka fau't;
Gin ye be ill, ye're, like mysel',
    Faith! as ill cau't.

But as yer fauts I've tauld, 'thout
    sparing,
Yer properties I'll too be sharing;
An' tell the warld the virtues glaring,
    O' Whisky guid,
Whilk fills our Sons wi' noble daring,
    An' warms their bluid.

Our Sodgers brave, inspir'd by thee,
Do charge their faes wi' as much glee,
As they were kemping on the lee,
    Whaur blinks loves charms;
Nae fear that they surpass'd should be,
    In deeds o' arms.

Auld Scotia's bairns, baith ane an' a',
Like weel wi' thee to weet their maw;
Through seas they'll dash, in frost an'
    sna',
    In fishing wherry,
Or tend their flocks whan keen win's
    blaw,
    An' be fu' merry.

Our Sons o' Learning an' the Arts,
By yer pure streams hae shawn their
    parts;
Ye clear their heads, an' warm their
    hearts,
    Gar them see better,
As lightening swift on Genius darts,
    Wi' dazzling glitter.

Ye aft inspire the self-taught Bard,
An' claim frae him his kind regard;
For aft ye are the sole reward,
    On him bestow'd;
Mair shame on them, whase heart's sae
    hard,
    Cou'd ease his load.

Our Music now's been lang admir'd;
Our Minstrels, sure, by you've been
    hir'd;
Yer cheering warmth, their hearts hae
    fir'd,
    Like Greek Apoll,
An' gar'd them sound their pipes,
    inspir'd
    By Alcohol.

E'en beggar bodies are fu' happy,
Whane'er o' ye they get a drappie,
In horn, or stoup, or timmer cappie,
    Tho' duds be scanty;
Yet blest as kings, they, owre the
    nappie,
    Forget ilk wantie.

But, what need further botheration,
I'm clear, a drap in moderation,
Has a' the wise's approbation;
    Then, guid Scots Whisky,
Mak' a' the bairns o' this auld nation
    'S leal hearts fu' frisky.

This is not the same George Bruce who wrote 'The Glass o' Whisky'. That George Bruce came from St Andrews, whereas this George Bruce was from Edinburgh. This poem is from his book 'Poems and Songs on Various Occasions' published in 1811.

Here's to You Again

ALEXANDER RODGER (1784-1846)

Let votaries o' Bacchus o' wine make their
   boast,
And drink till it mak' them as dead's a
   bed-post;
A drap o' maut broe I wad far rather pree,
And a rosy-faced landlord's the Bacchus
   for me.
Then I'll toddle but and I'll toddle ben,
And let them drink at wine wha nae better
   do ken.

Your wine it may do for the bodies far
   south,
But a Scotsman likes something that bites i'
   the mouth,
And whisky's the thing that can do't to a tee.
Then Scotsmen and whisky will ever agree;
For wi' toddlin' but and toddlin' ben,
Sae lang we've been nurst on't we hardly can
   spean.

It's now thretty years since I first took the
   drap,
To moisten my carcase and keep it in sap;
And though what I've drunk might hae
   slacken'd the sun,
I find I'm as dry as when first I begun;
For wi' toddlin' but and toddlin' ben,
I'm nae sooner slacken'd than drouthy
   again.

Your douse folk aft ca' me a tipplin' auld
   sot,
A worm to a still, a sand-bed, and what
   not;
They cry that my hand wad ne'er bide frae
   my mouth;
But, oddsake! They never consider my
   drouth;
Yet I'll toddle but and I'll toddle ben,
An' laugh at their nonsense wha nae better
   ken.

Some hard-grippin' mortals wha deem
   themselves wise,
A glass o' gude whisky affect to despise;
Poor scurvy-soul'd wretches, they're no very
   blate,
Besides, let me tell them, they're foes to the
   state;
For wi' toddlin but and toddlin' ben,
Gin folk wadna drink, how could
   government fen'?

Yet wae on the tax that maks whisky sae
   dear,
An' wae on the gauger sae strict and severe;
Had I but my will o't, I'd soon let you see,
That whisky, like water, to a' should be free;
For I'd toddle but and I'd toddle ben,
And I'd mak it rin like the burn after rain.

What signifies New'r day? - a mock at the
    best,
That tempts but poor bodies and leaves
    them unblest?
For ance-a-year fuddle I'd scarce gie a strae,
Unless that ilk year were as short as a day;
Then I'd toddle but and I'd toddle ben,
Wi' the hearty het pint and the canty black
    hen.

I ne'er was inclined to lay-by ony cash,
Weel kennin' it only wad breed me more
    fash;
But aye when I had it I let it gang free,
And wad toss for a gill wi' my hindmost
    bawbee;
For wi' toddlin' but and toddlin' ben,
I ne'er kent the use o't but only to spen'.

Had siller been made in the kist to lock by,
It ne'er wad been rund, but square as a die;
Whereas by its shape ilka body may see,
It aye was designed it should circulate free;
Then we'll toddle but and we'll toddle ben,
An' aye when we get it, we'll part wi't again.

I ance was persuaded to 'put in the pin,'
But foul fa' the bit o't ava wad bide in;
For whisky's a thing sae bewitchingly stout,
The first time I smelt it the pin it lap out;
Then I toddled but and I toddled ben,
And I vow'd I wad ne'er be advised sae again.

Oh, leeze me on whisky! It gie's us new life,
It maks us aye cadgy to cuddle the wife;
It kindles a spark in the breast o' the cauld,
And it maks the rank coward courageously
    bauld;
Then we'll toddle but and we'll toddle ben,
An' we'll coup aff our glasses, 'Here's to you
    again!'

There are some fantastic lines in this whisky panegyric. 'Maks us aye cadgy to cuddle the wife' shows that, even in the 19th century, some people realised the viagric power of whisky. Who could therefore disagree that 'whisky, like water, to a' should be free'?

Campbeltown Loch

ANDY STEWART

Oh, Campbeltown Loch, I wish ye were whisky,
Campbeltown Loch, Och aye,
Campbeltown Loch, I wish ye were whisky,
I wad drink ye dry.

Now Campbeltown Loch is a beautifiul place
But the price o' the whisky is grim.
How nice it would be, if the whisky was free,
And the loch was full up tae the brim.

Oh, Campbeltown Loch, &c.

I'd buy a wee yacht, wi' the money I've got,
And I'd anchor it oot in the bay.
If I wanted a nip, I'd go in for a dip,
I'd be divin' an' dookin' a' day.

Oh, Campbeltown Loch, &c.

But what if my boat, it should overturn,
And drowned in the whisky was I;
You'd hear me shout, you would hear me call out,
'What a wonderful way to die'.

Oh, Campbeltown Loch, &c.

This song became extremely popular in the 1960s. It was written by Andy Stewart, singer and comedian and writer of 'Donald, Whaur's Your Troosers'.

The story of the decline of Campbeltown as a whisky-making region is one of the sad chapters in the history of Scotch whisky.

Incidentally, Campbeltown Loch is a sea-loch, so this must win the prize for the biggest amount of whisky in any fantasy.

A Wee Drap o' Whisky

TRADITIONAL

A wee drap o' whisky I tak' when I'm weary
My blood for to warm and my spirits to
   cheer
And when I sit doon I intend to be merry
So fill up a bumper and bring it round
   here.

I can scarce get a hauf oor when I am weary
To tell you the truth I am wrocht very sore
My ploo and my lassie are a' my whole
   pleasure
We'll baith tak' a kiss an' hae a drap mair.

Contented I sit and contented I labour
Contented I drink and contented I sing
I never dispute nor fa' oot wi' my neebors
For that is a mean and contentious thing.

Oh few, very few ever hear me compleenin'
Though oftimes the load of oppression I
   bear
Oh fat is the use o' a man aye compleenin'
For aye fan he tastes, he maun hae a drap
   mair.

Come noble waiter, bring in a large
   measure,
I mean hauf a mutchkin, the best o' the
   toon
An' when it is drunken, it's time to be
   joggin
Wi' the lightest o' care we'll gang toddlin'
   hame.

So good night to you all, I think it's nae
   treason,
Altho' that the whisky speaks saft in my ear
Good night and safe home, till further
   occasion
We'll a' meet in friendship and hae a drap
   mair.

The ploughman singing this song is clearly a fellow who favours moderation and self-control. Be that as it may, he is still moved to sing the praises of a simple life and the place of whisky in that existence.

What a Mischief Whisky's Done

IN DISPRAISE OF WHISKY

Needless to say, the disapproving section of the community are quite capable of expressing their opinions in poems and songs. These rantings and railings range from very powerful poems and effective songs to some absolute drivel. Mostly they were created and promoted by the Temperance movement.

Religious disapproval of whisky reached a high point in the 19th and early 20th centuries. The Temperance movement was incredibly powerful and pervasive. In 1850, for example, there were 26,000 members of the Rechabites in Lanarkshire alone and that was only one of the Temperance organisations seeking a complete ban on strong alcohol. The Temperance League was perhaps the biggest of these organisations in Scotland. This was truly a mass movement. The members were largely women and children (though by no means all). Rallies were held in places like the common land near Arthur's Seat in Edinburgh and train loads of children would be shipped in from all over the country. Thousands would gather to sing songs and hear speeches against the evil of drink.

As a result of pressure from the Temperance lobby, Scotland held local plebiscites (or referenda) just before the First World War, and many areas voted to be dry. Places like Wick and Stromness had an alcohol ban for 25 years (implemented after the War). Kilsyth and Kirkintilloch only repealed the by-law in the 1970s. Though it was not country-wide, this was a longer prohibition than that suffered by the USA. Few people now realise or can grasp the scale of the Temperance movement in Scotland at that time. Fortunately, good sense prevailed, there is only the slightest vestige of restriction left, like not being able to buy alcohol on a Sunday morning.

Religious disapproval tends to produce an opposite reaction in some people. Either because they resist structures of authority (and there is something of the liberation fighter in the Scots character), or because they do not like to be told what to do. It's like the 'paradoxical injunction' which can work so well with children – if you want them to do something, forbid them to do it and watch it get done. Whatever the reason, in any Scottish street you can find the teetotaller and the 'death wish' drinker living in the same close.

It difficult to know whether the Temperance movement was a reaction to excessive alcohol consumption (they certainly perceived that to be the case), or whether excessive alcohol consumption was a reaction to the irritating zeal and moral high-handedness of the Temperance brigade and the church in general. Perhaps the truth has a bit of both sides wrapped up in it.

When Johnnie Was Gi'en to the Weeting His Mou'

DAVID BROWN (1826-1886)

When Johnnie was gi'en to the weeting his mou'
Our dwalling was scantily plenish'd enow:
A slave to the whisky, for *it* but he wrought,
And how to get mair o't was a' that he thought;
As he staucher'd but, and he staucher'd ben,
And what he was doing did scarce ever ken.

The laird would aft grumble and gloom for his rent;
The young anes be girning and greeting for want;
Their backs were ill-clad, and their bellies were toom;
But Johnnie gat fou', and 'twas a' ane to him:
For he staucher'd but, and he staucher'd ben,
Regardless o' landlord, o' wife, or o' wean.

O mony a lang night, wi' a tear in my e'e,
Nae fire in the grate, and the bairn on my knee,
I've waited on Johnnie when out at the dram;
For ne'er could I rest till I saw him come hame:
Then he'd staucher but, and he'd staucher ben,
Or sleep but to wake and cry, 'Whisky' again.

My heart was sae broken, sae dreary my life,
It seem'd as a' Nature and I were at strife;
The vera day-light that gave a' besides glee,
Dawn'd only to darken Creation to me;
As he staucher'd but, and he staucher'd ben,
I aften maist wish'd my existence wad en'.

But Gude bless the Temp'rance, for ay since he join'd,
My life is sae alter'd - my Johnnie's sae kind;
Our bien house and bairns are his pleasure and pride,
Contented he sits at his ain ingle side.
Now I'm happy but, and I'm happy ben,
And think but to smile on the days that are gane.

O wae upon liquors, the strong and the sma',
An' wae upon whisky - the warst o' them a';
They ca' it a *spirit* - weel sae they may do;
And mony ha'e found it an *evil* ane too;
But we'll banish the fiend to his ain wicked den,
Syne plenty and peace o'er the warld shall reign!

'Wae upon whisky - the warst o' them a''.
Don't these temperance poems give you an immediate thirst!
This song should be compared with 'Here's to You Again', which has the same tune but a
completely contradictory message.

What a Mischief Whisky's Done

TRADITIONAL

What a mischief whisky's done
Gar't mony a one stark naked run
And wi' his nose to shiel the grun'
As he is goin' hame O.

Weary on the gill stoup
The gill stoup, the gill stoup
My curse upon the gill stoup
Brings muckle grief at hame O.

Drunken Jake he's no much better
He drinks the whisky like cold water
And then he sets oot like a hatter
Oot owre the ragin' main O.

Souter Jock, the ither day
Gaed doon the toon tae draw his pay
He met wi' drunken Sauny Grey
Brocht nae a bawbee hame O.

My gudeman gaed to the mill
Gaed to the mill to buy some meal
The miller he being at the gill
They saul the sack gaun hame O.

The lasses think they are nae richt
While they lie doon their lanes at nicht
And day and nicht their fancies flicht
Sayin' how'll we get a man O.

Where on earth can a woman find a decent man, when their heads are so easily turned by the sound of a cork being pulled? This song was obviously written by a disgruntled wife. Maybe she, and the other frustrated lassies in the last verse, should just console themselves with a wee dram.

The Demon Drink

WILLIAM McGONAGALL (1830-1902)

Oh, thou demon Drink, thou fell destroyer;
Thou curse of society, and its great annoyer.
What hast thou done to society, let me think?
I answer thou hast caused the most of ills, thou demon Drink.

Thou causeth the mother to neglect her child,
Also the father to act as he were wild,
So that he neglects his loving wife and family dear,
By spending his earnings foolishly on whisky, rum and beer.

After spending his earnings foolishly he beats his wife-
The man that promised to protect her during life-
And so the man would if there was no drink in society,
For seldom a man beats his wife in a state of sobriety.

And if he does, perhaps he finds his wife fou',
Then that causes, no doubt, a great hullabaloo;
When he finds his wife drunk he begins to frown,
And in a fury of passion he knocks her down.

And in the knock down she fractures her head,
And perhaps the poor wife is killed dead,
Whereas, if there was no strong drink to be got,
To be killed wouldn't have been the poor woman's lot.

Then the unfortunate husband is arrested and cast into jail,
And sadly his fate he does bewail;
And he curses the hour that ever he was born,
And paces his cell up and down very forlorn.

And when the day of his trial draws near,
No doubt for the murdering of his wife he drops a tear,
And he exclaims, 'Oh, thou demon Drink, through thee I must die,'
And on the scaffold he warns the people from drink to fly,

Because whenever a father or a mother takes to drink,
Step by step on in crime they do sink,
Until their children loses all affection for them,
And in justice we cannot their children condemn.

The man that gets drunk is little else than a fool,
And is in the habit, no doubt, of advocating for Home Rule;
But the best Home Rule for him, as far as I can understand,
Is the abolition of strong drink from the land.

And the men that get drunk in general wants Home Rule;
But such men, I rather think, should keep their heads cool,
And try and learn more sense, I most earnestly do pray,
And help to get strong drink abolished without delay.

If drink was abolished how many peaceful homes would there be,
Just, for instance, in the beautiful town of Dundee;
Then this world would be a heaven, whereas it's a hell,
And the people would have more peace in it to dwell.

Alas! Strong drink makes men and women fanatics,
And helps to fill our prisons and lunatics;
And if there was no strong drink such cases wouldn't be,
Which would be a very glad sight for all Christians to see.

I admit a man may be a very good man,
But in my opinion he cannot be a true Christian
As long as he partakes of strong drink,
The more that he may differently think.

But no matter what he thinks, I say nay,
For by taking it he helps to lead his brother astray,
Whereas, if he didn't drink, he would help to reform society,
And we would soon do away with all inebriety.

Then, for the sake of society and the Church of God,
Let each one try to abolish it at home and abroad;
Then poverty and crime would decrease and be at a stand,
And Christ's Kingdom would soon be established throughout the land.

Therefore, brothers and sisters, pause and think,
And try to abolish the foul fiend, Drink.
Let such doctrine be taught in church and school,
That the abolition of strong drink is the only Home Rule.

This is one of McGonagall's temperance poems. Another is called 'A New Temperance Poem for my Departed Parents, Who Were Sober Living and Godfearing People'. The thing about McGonagall is that his poems are so bad that they can be quite entertaining, especially read aloud.

He was a man with a mission and would go round the pubs of Edinburgh and Dundee hawking his poems. With messages like this in his poems, he was probably thrown out of more pubs than your average penniless alcoholic. I love the assertion that drunkards would be likely to support Home Rule!

Tee-Total Song

TRADITIONAL

My wife and I, when we were wed,
Had routh o' every thing we needit;
Our meat an' claes we duly paid,
An' landlords visits never dreaded.
Morn cam', an' wi' the lark we raise,
An' eidently we toiled thegither,
While blyth Content learned in our hame,
That Industry was Plenty's mither.

Night cam', and ere we gaed to rest,
We sat and talked o' prospects cheering;
Syne, fand in slumber's silken faulds,
The joys to labour sae endearing.
To keep the weans baith clean and braw,
Was aye my thrifty wifie's pleasure;
And on their buiks she'd *'targe them tight,'*
Whene'er she had a moment's leisure.

Respect did aye our steps attend,
Our weel won gear was aye increasing:
Nae morning rase without its joys;
Ilk e'ening brought with it a blessing.
But waes my heart that I should tell't,
A neighbour lad set up a change house;
And O! It had been weel for me,
If I had made it, still, a strange house.

But I, wi' mony mae gaed there,
To hear and tell some clishmaclavers;
An' cracks ye ken, without a gill,
Are fushonless lang-winded havers.
And things just a beginning need,
And sae it fared wi' our carousing,
For soon it turned frae ance a-week,
To a hail week o' dounright bousing.

Night cam', and at the club we met,
We aye grew fonder o' each ither;
Ilk gill fresh disputation brought,
To settle which we ca'd anither:
Morn cam', and found us in our beds,
Wi' parched tongues and three-fourths
    crazy,
Wi' bluid-red eyes and aching heads,
An' spirits sair depressed and hazy.

Our feeble knees, our shrunken frames,
Our state to neighbours was revealing,
And sober men would shun our path,
As if we had been ken't for stealing.
Wark gaed ahin'; our hard won gear
Took wings, an' we had nought to live on,
Our credit dwindled wi' our claes,
An' left us emptiness to grieve on.

Our bairns frae being trig and braw,
Turned ragged, lean, an' heedless
    creatures;
Our vexed wives laid by their smiles,
An' discontent possessed their features.

I saw the wreck that I had made,
An' often cursed my reckless folly,
An' aften swore I'd be reformed,
An' give up drinking spirits wholly.

Yet still at night I'd to the club,
To hear what news my frien's had gathered;
Where ae glass o' the ruin *blue*,
Me in the magic circle tethered.
At length remorse cam to my aid,
An' mildly sketched my late condition,
An' urged me to forsake my ways,
Which lead directly to perdition.

A retrospective glance displayed,
My wife an' weans ance bien an' happy,
Now to the brink o' ruin brought,
Bacause I wadna want the drappie.
Conviction flashed upon my mind,
A sense of shame stole slowly o'er me,
A film dropt from my eyes; I saw
The loathsome way which stretched before
 me.

I fled – I sought my ruined hame,
I called on stern resolve to aid me;
An' from that hour I ne'er touch'd drink,
Nor will again till judgement fade me.

My house again' is clean an' trig,
My wifie has resumed her smiling,
My weans are everything I wish,
An' I ne'er tire o' honest toiling.
Then learn frae me, ye thoughtless fools,
Wha think ye're happiness pursuing,
To seek it at your ain firesides,
And strive to do as I am doing.

We don't know what happened in the four missing lines of the penultimate verse. A tantalising gap, but it does not affect the flow of the story. 'Blue' is an old Scots word for whisky – sometimes called 'blue nappy'. I don't know where the word comes from, but there is a definite blue tint in whisky straight from the still.

A Mither's Lecture Tae Her Ne'er-dae-weel Son

CHARLES NICOL (1858 - ?)

Ye thochtless tyke, what time o' nicht
Is this for tae come hame?
Whan ither decent fouk's in bed -
Oh! div ye no think shame?
But shame's no in ye, that I ken,
Ye drucken ne'er-dae-weel!
You've mair thocht for the dram-shop
    there -
Aye, that ye hae, atweel!

Ye drucken loon, come tell me quick
Whaur hae ye been, ava?
I'm shair it's waefu' that frae drink
Ye canna keep awa.
An' bidin' tae sic 'oors as this,
When you should be in bed;
I doot there's something in this wark;
Come, tell the truth noo, Ted?

Can ye no speak? What's wrang wi' ye?
Ye good-for-naething loon,
Yer gettin' juist a fair disgrace,
An' that ye'll be gey soon.
Noo, dinna stan' there like a mute -
The truth I want tae ken,
Sae tell me noo the truth for aince,
It's nae too late tae men'.

You've been wi' twa-three bosom freens
At Bob Broon's birthday spree;
Aweel, aweel, if *that's* the case,
You this time I'll forgie.
But mind, sic wark as this, my man,
Will never, never dae;
Ye maun gie up that waefu' drink,
Aye, frae this very day!

65

The Barley Bree

TRADITIONAL

Oor auld guidman gaed to the toon, to sell
  his puckle woo';
And he cam' back withoot a plack, his
  noddle reevin' fou;
And on the road he lost his wig, as black as
  ony slae,
Besides a plaid I span mysel', the best o'
  hodden gray.

*Oh, weary on the barley bree, that brings baith scaith
  and scorn;*
*It mak's us tyne oor peace o' min', and wish we'd ne'er
  been born.*

Wi' fearfu' bang he oped the door, syne
  clashed doon by the fire;
His troosers split frae heid tae fit, his han's
  a' owre wi' mire;
His cheeks were scarted right and left, wi'
  fa'in amo' the whins;
His nose had come against a stane, and he
  had peel'd his shins.

Oh, weary on the barley bree, &c.

Wae's me, I cried, I never thocht that I
  would live to see
My ain guidman in sic a plight, - is this
  your love to me!
Is this a wye to treat a wife, wha lo'es ye day
  and nicht;
The bairns are greetin' in their beds, I'm
  maist near deid wi' fricht!

Oh, weary on the barley bree, &c.

It's haud your tongue and dinna speak, but
  keep as quate's a moose,
Or I'll tak' and brak' your backs, and syne
  I'll fire the hoose.
Wi' that he tummlet aff the cheer, and fell
  doon on the rug;
And there he lay till mornin' gray aside the
  collie dog.

Oh, weary on the barley bree, &c.

I sleepit nane that leelang nicht, my he'rt
    was like to brak';
But there he lay wi' baith his han's firm
    clasped roon collie's neck.

Oh, weary on the barley bree, &c.

But noo it's altered days, I trow, I'm
    happier than a queen,
For ilka day's as blithe as May; we're gettin'
    snug and bien.
And hoo this change has come aboot,
    I trow ye'll maybe guess, -
Oor Robin's turned teetotaler, and winna
    taste a gless.

Oh, weary on the barley bree, &c.

*This is one of the few songs to raise the
possibility of violence resulting from whisky
drinking. Sure enough, if that happened
you might decide to give it up - or else
choose a better whisky. Some consider grain
whiskies (and therefore blended whiskies)
to be more likely to have such unwanted
side-effects than pure malt.*

Nancy's Whisky

TRADITIONAL

I'm a weaver and I follow the weaving
I'm a young and a rovin' blade,
And to buy myself a suit of clothing
Down to Stewarton my way I made.

As I cam' roond by Stewarton corner
Nancy's whisky I did spy,
Says I tae myself, I think I'll try some,
It's seven lang years now I have been dry.

Oh the whisky, aye the whisky,
Nancy's whisky, whisky oh.

The more I tried it, the more I liked it,
The more I liked it, I tasted more;
And the more I tasted, the more I liked it,
'Til a' my senses had gone ashore.

Early, early, the very next morning,
I wakened up in a stranger's bed.
I tried to rise but I wasnae able,
Nancy's whisky held doon my head.

Oh the whisky, &c.

I went up tae the dour landlady,
And asked her how much I had to pay;
She said 'your reckoning is thirty shillings,
So pay me quickly and get on your way'.

I put my hand intae my pocket,
And all I had I laid it doon;
Efter payin' the thirty shillings
A' that was left was a poor half-croon.

Oh the whisky, &c.

As I cam oot and I turned the corner
A charming lassie I did spy;
Me an' her, we spent twa shillings
And a' that's left now is a crooked boy.

I'll gang hame and I'll start weaving
And my wee shuttles, I'll mak' them flee
And curses be on Nancy's whisky
For Nancy's whisky has ruined me.

Oh the whisky, &c.

This is the version sung by Willie Scott. The young man made at least one fundamental mistake – not having had a dram for seven years he was out of practise.

The Corries did a version of this song in which the young man wakes up in bed beside a horrible, ugly, smelly old woman. He tries to escape but she insists on payment for her services the night before, which gratefully he can't remember. He finds that most of his money is gone and he is mortified to confess that he only has six–pence. 'That's all right, son', she says, 'I've plenty change'.

Rosie Stewart sang me an Irish version which is exactly the same as this one until the last verse, when the young man proclaims that he is going back to work to earn more money – so he can do it all again next week. Tells you something about the difference between our attitude to whisky and that of the Irish.

There is a female version of the song called 'Johnny Whisky'.

John Barleycorn, my Jo

GEORGE BARRON (19th Century)

John Barleycorn, my jo John when we were
first acquaint
I had money in my pocket John but noo, ye
ken I want
I spent it all in treating John because I loved
you so
And look ye how you've cheated me John
Barleycorn my jo.

John Barleycorn, my jo John, one of your
many ills
You rob me of my money John which
ought to pay my bills
My creditors upbraid me John why I do use
them so
Which is the cruellest thing ava John
Barleycorn my jo.

John Barleycorn, my jo John, beside your
other evils
You threatened, Sir, to frighten me by
raising your blue devils
Sic company I dinna like John frae the
regions down below
So dinna try sic tricks again John
Barleycorn my jo.

John Barleycorn, my jo John, of friends ye
hae sae many
But surely ye hae nae forgot on drunken
Peter Rennie
For mony's the merry nicht we've had in
sunshine and in snow
But we three maun ne'er meet again John
Barleycorn my jo.

It's true he will forswear you for longer
time or shorter
For often you do gang to him disguised as
Mr. Porter
Sic tricks I dinna like John they are so mean
and low
I wad rather see you naked far John
Barleycorn my jo.

And in the early morning John before that
I get up
I would take you in a tumbler John and
gladly drink you up
We are told to love our enemies John and
why should it not be so
That we take our last and farewell glass John
Barleycorn my jo.

You are surely turning frail John, when
friends upon you call
Unless it be at certain hours you can't be
seen at all
And likewise upon Sunday John your face
you winna show
Unless to some particular folks John
Barleycorn my jo.

But we will never miss you John suppose ye
keep your bed
For we've plenty of lay preachers in the
country in your stead
Wha deals the spirit largely alike to rich and
low
I hope that it will stand the proof John
Barleycorn my jo.

And at the feeing markets John, on you we'll
turn our backs
And we will treat the lasses John to Peter
Drummond's tracts
Who will receive them gladly John and read
them as they go
Your days are numbered now on earth John
Barleycorn my jo.

This seems to be a song sung by a man who has recently discovered the error of his ways, but it is heavy with ambivalence and a swithering of resolve. Apparently George Barron was a shoemaker who 'composed his poetry when drunk and swore at it when sober'. There is a wonderful irony, if not tortuous logic, in this somewhere.

However, if the shoemaker thinks the lasses at the feeing markets would prefer Peter Drummond's tracts to John Barleycorn, then maybe it's his mental state that is in question, rather than his sobriety.

Tam Maut

JOHN BARR (1822-1892)

Drunken Tam Maut's gane awa' to the
    toon,
His sense and his siller in liquor to droon,
And he winna come back till he's in the
    blue deils,
Seein' cats and red monkeys wi' spurs on
    their heels:

When Drunken Tam Maut gets ance on the
    spree,
He'll fecht wi' the wind, or he'll fecht wi' a
    flee,
He'll roar, curse, and swear, without sense
    or shame,
And he caresna a feg for his wife or his
    hame.

Then he'll roar out for drink to slocken his
    drouth,
Wi' his teeth set on edge, and the foam at
    his mouth,
Then he'll dance roun' the room wi' a
    whoop and a yell,
But that's reckoned naething when Tam's
    on the gell.

His breakfast is whisky, his dinner's the
    same,
And he taks it for supper, to smother his
    shame;
Then he lies in his bed like a lump o' deid
    clay,
And he roars out for drink by the first
    screigh o' day.

As his senses gang oot, then the deevil
    comes in,
And ye'll ken it's Tam Maut by his roarin'
    and din;
There's a crood at the door for they're
    turnin' him oot,
And he lands in the dirt as he's wheelin'
    aboot.

Noo drunken Tam Maut has gane hame to
    his wife,
He has broken her heart and embittered
    her life;
But what cares Tam Maut for man, wife or
    wean,
He has noo dune his warst, and his judge-
    ment is gane.

Noo he'll rage through the house like a bull
in a ring,
Then he'll sit down and greet, then he'll
jump up and sing;
Then he'll gang to his bed, but he'll no sleep
a wink,
For his brain is on fire wi' the fumes o' the
drink.

Noo he'll jump oot o' bed, swear the deil's
in the house,
Tho' it's naething ava but the squeak o' a
mouse;
But there's deil eneugh there when Tam's in
it himsel',
For he's noo in confab wi' the demons o'
hell.

Cauld sweat noo in torrents pour down his
pale face,
And 'tis plain to be seen he has finished his
race;
He pants noo for breath, and he clutches his
hair,
Death closes the scene, and he dies in
despair.

Puir drunken Tam Maut's noo laid in his
grave,
He wisna a thief, nor was he a knave;
And yet he was waur, for wi' drinkin' and
strife,
He cheated himsel' and he shortened his
life.

My God, what a cautionary tale! If you ever happen to see red monkeys wi' spurs on their heel, you may just have gone too far.

To Mak a Body Strong

THE CURATIVE POWER OF WHISKY?

In Scotland a tremendous mythology has grown up about the medicinal property of whisky. Whisky toddy for colds, whisky for palsy, melancholy, ring worms, spots on the face. As 'the cure for which there is no disease', whisky has been the Scottish version of Prozac for hundreds of years. According to Tobias Smollett, the highlanders gave it to their children to prevent them catching smallpox — maybe liver failure was more of a problem. My old granny kept a bottle, purely for 'medicinal purposes'. She took a drop when she was anxious, depressed, worried, tired or feeling out of sorts to name but a few of her frequent ailments.

Of course, the idea of whisky as a positive, curative thing with beneficial, medicinal effect is a convenient way of making it respectable to have and to drink. It is a way round the religious disapproval. Interestingly, there may be a grain of truth in it. Recent research has shown that a certain amount of alcohol is good for you — reduces stress and benefits the heart and the circulation. The difficulty, as always, is to get the experts to agree on what is a proper amount. James Hogg once said that 'if a man could just find oot the exact, proper quantity that should be taken every day, and stick to that, I verily trow that he might live for ever — withoot dyin' at a', and that doctors and kirkyairds would go oot o' fashion.' That may have been a wee bit of an exaggeration, but the idea is sound. There is no doubt in my mind that whisky, far more than cannabis, has a claim to be classified as a prescription drug which should be available on the NHS. For people who need relaxation, stress reduction or general loosening up, for palliative care, for mild anaesthetic and for all those folk who really just need an interest, social stimulation — a life.

No doubt it would be argued in opposition that too much whisky is harmful. True it can be — but then there are very few prescription drugs that are not also harmful if you take too much. This is not really the problem; the problem is that it doesn't seem right to some people to have a drug that is also enjoyable! How my granny used to screw her face up when she had to take her medicine.

Drinkin' Drams

(The Tippler's Progress)

GEORGE OUTRAM (1805-1856)

He ance was holy
An' melancholy,
Till he found the folly
  O singin' psalms
He's now red's a rose,
And there's pimples on his nose,
And in size it daily grows
  By drinkin' drams.

He ance was weak,
And couldnae eat a steak
Wi'out gettin' sick
  An' takin' qualms;
But now he can eat
O ony kind o' meat
For he's got an appeteet
  By drinkin' drams.

He ance was thin,
Wi' a nose like a pen,
An' haunds like a hen,
  An' nae hams;
But now he's round and tight,
And a deevil o' a wight,
For he's got himsel' put right
  By drinkin' drams.

He ance was soft as dirt,
As pale as ony shirt,
And as useless as a cart
  Wi'out the trams;
But now he'd race the deil,
Or swallow Jonah's whale–
He's as gleg's a puddock's tail
  Wi' drinkin' drams.

Oh! Pale, pale was his hue,
And cauld, cauld was his broo,
An' he grumbled like a ewe
  'Mang libbit rams;
But noo his broo is bricht,
An' his een are orbs o' licht,
An' his nose is just a sicht
  Wi' drinkin' drams.

He studied mathematics,
Logic, ethics, hydrostatics,
Till he needed diuretics
  To louse his dams;
But now wi'out a lee,
He could mak' anither sea,
For he's left philosophy
  An' ta'en to drams.

He found that learnin', fame,
Gas, philanthropy and steam,
Logic, loyalty, gude name,
  Were a' mere shams;
That the source o' joy below,
An' the antidote to woe,
And the only proper go,
  Was drinkin' drams.

It's true that we can see
Auld Nick wi' gloatin' ee,
Just waitin' till he dee
  'Mid frichts and dwams;
But what's Auld Nick to him,
Or palsied tongue or limb,
Wi' glass filled to the brim
  When drinkin' drams!

Shows how whisky can transform your existence, in unimaginable ways – why else is it called the Water of Life?

Ballade of good whisky

NORMAN MacCAIG (1910-1996)

You whose ambition is to swim the Minch
Or write a drum concerto in B flat
Or run like Bannister or box like Lynch
Or find the Ark wrecked on Mt Ararat -
No special training's needed: thin or fat,
You'll do it if you never once supplant
As basis of your commissariat
Glenfiddich, Bruichladdich and
   Glengrant.

My own desires are small. In fact, I flinch
From heaving a heavenly Hindu from her
   ghat
Or hauling Loch Ness monsters, inch by
   inch,
Out of their wild and watery habitat.
I've no desire to be Jehoshaphat
Or toy with houris fetched from the
   Levant.
But give to me — *bis dat qui cito dat* —
Glenfiddich, Bruichladdich and
   Glengrant.

I would drink down, and think the feat a
   cinch,
The Congo, Volga, Amazon, La Platte,
And Tweed as chaser - a bargain, this, to
   clinch
In spite of *nota bene* and *caveat*
(Though what a feast must follow after that
Of Amplex, the divine deodorant!)
If they ran — hear my heart go pit-a-pat! —
Glenfiddich, Bruichladdich and
   Glengrant.

Envoi
Chris! (whether perpendicular or flat
Or moving rather horribly aslant)
Here is a toast that you won't scunner at —
Glenfiddich, Bruichladdich and
   Glengrant!

One of the great poets of the Twentieth Century, MacCaig often avoided rhyming. This example, however, shows he could be a master of rhyme. Again the message is that with good malt whisky, you can do great things. I like the rivers of whisky in the third verse. I guess the envoi is addressed to Chris Grieve (Hugh MacDiarmid).

Piper MacNeil

TRADITIONAL

Ye'll a' hae heard o' Piper MacNeil
A canty chap and a coothie chiel,
And a' my days Ah lo'ed him weel
For he dearly lo'ed the whisky-o.

The whisky's guid, aye the whisky's grand,
A wee drappie o't'll dae ye nae harm,
An' Ah only wish that in my airms
Ah had a great big barrel o' Hielan whisky-o.

When Ah cam staggerin' hame ae nicht
As fou as ony man could be,
Ah struck a post an' doon Ah fell
Jist wi' a wee drappie whisky-o.

The whisky's guid, &c.

When Ah cam staggerin' up tae the door
Ma mither rase an' she slipped the bar,
But when she saw ma claes a' glar
She said 'Curse tae the Hielan whisky-o'.

The whisky's guid, &c.

Now mither ye needna angry be
And intae a passion, dinna flee,
For aye until the day Ah dee
Ah'll aye tak a wee drappie whisky-o.

The whisky's guid, &c.

I'm not quite sure what this song is about, but the message seems to be 'Whisky is good for you, so I am going to drink it as long as I can, whatever disapproving people might say – and by the way, I wish I had a huge quantity of it right now.' I'll drink to that!

Old Wife in High Spirits

In an Edinburgh Pub

HUGH MacDIARMID (1892-1978)

An auld wumman cam' in, a mere rickle o'
    banes, in a faded black dress
And a bonnet wi' beads o' jet rattlin' on it;
A puir-lookin' cratur, you'd think she could
    haurdly ha'e had less
Life left in her and still lived, but dagonit!

He gied her a stiff whisky - she was nervous
    as a troot
And could haurdly haud the tumbler, puir
    cratur;
Syne he gied her anither, joked wi' her, and
    anither, and syne
Wild as the whisky up cam' her nature.

The rod that struck water frae the rock in
    the desert
Was naething to the life that sprang oot o'
    her;
The dowie auld soul was twinklin' and fizzin'
    wi' fire;
You never saw ocht sae souple and kir.

Like a sackful o' monkeys she was, and her
    lauchin'
Loupit up whiles to incredible heights;
Wi' ane owre the eight her temper changed
    and her tongue
Flew juist as the forkt lichtnin' skites.

The heich skeich auld cat was fair in her ele-
    ment;
Wanton as a whirlwind, and shairly better
    that way
Than a' crippen thegither wi' laneliness and
    cauld
Like a foretaste o' the graveyaird clay.

Some folk nae doot'll condemn gie'in' a
    guid spree
To the puir dune body and raither she endit
    her days
Like some auld tashed copy o' the Bible yin
    sees
On a street book-barrow's tipenny trays,

A' I ken is weel-fed and weel-put-on
    though they be
Ninety percent o' respectable folk never hae
As muckle life in their creeshy carcasses frae
    beginnin' to end
As kythed in that wild auld carline that day!

Another auld wife rejuvenated by the water of life! MacDiarmid had an enormous respect for Scotland's national drink. His most famous comments about it are to be found in the opening stanzas of his poem 'A Drunk Man Looks at the Thistle'.

Cripple Kirsty

TRADITIONAL

It's wha amang ye hisna heard o' weel-kent
    Cripple Kirsty
A porter met her in the street and spiert gin
    she wis thirsty.
'Oh yes indeed, an' that I am' she smirkin'
    said fu' pawkie
'And gin ye'll lay yer tippence tae mine we'll
    hae a wee drap whisky.'

Sing Fal the dal etc. etc.

Quo he 'Wi me noo wark is scant an' siller
    isnae plenty
Yet when a mornin's caul' and wet to join I
    am content aye'
Sae he drew tippence frae his spunge a
    spunge made o' a cat skin
An' ower to Shirra's baith they gied an'
    called for half-a-mutchkin.

Kirsty smellt it ere she took her tift an' said
    'twas gweed, she houpit
Syne turnt her fingers to the lift an' Lanrick
    wise did coup it –
'Well done' quo he – 'Fill up' qho she 'An
    lat us hae some mair o't'
'Na! Na!' quo he 'ye greedy jade I think
    ye've got yer share o't.'

'A weel – a weel if that's the cure then I
    maun be contentit
But faith it's done me muckle gweed for I
    had nearly faintit.'
An' noo I hope ye'se gies a ca' some
    mornin' fin yer thirsty
An' as ye gae by the Fiddler's Close cry in
    for Cripple Kirsty.

Kirsty was obviously a woman who appreciated the curative power of whisky. It certainly revived her and set her up for the day. You wonder if she had been able to afford another whether it might have cured her disability altogether and had her dancing. 'Lanrick', in other songs, is a way of saying Lanark. What the expression 'Lanrick wise' means I do not know, but it clearly means downed in a oner.

The Hielan' Hills

TRADITIONAL

The Hielan' hills are high high
The Hielan' miles are long
But Hielan' whisky is the thing
To mak a body strong.

She'll tak a glass - be ne'en the waur
An' maybe she'll tak twa
An' if she should tak six or five
What business that tae you.

Her cuttie pipe is no that bad
To warm a body's nose
And Hielan' whisky is the thing
To paint it like the rose.

I'd like to know who 'she' was. A woman who takes a few drams and smokes a cuttie pipe could be an interesting companion!

The Morning After

STRATH CLAGUE

I don't feel too healthy this morning
with the whisky fumes still in my head.
No, I don't feel too healthy this morning
so I think I'll just stay here in bed.

Perhaps later today I'll feel better,
and maybe by late afternoon,
when my hands have stopped trembling and shaking,
I'll be able to eat.... With a spoon!

Then later on, in the evening,
I'll be back to normal, I think.
In fact I'll be feeling so healthy,
I might just go out for a drink.

Naturally, one of the most common medicinal uses for whisky is 'the hair of the dog'. *Strath once told me that he only ever drinks whisky when he's feeling ill – but he always* *takes enough to ensure he needs the remedy again the next day!*

Hughie's Winter Excuse for a Dram

HUGH HALIBURTON (JAMES LOGIE ROBERTSON) 1846-1922

Frae whaur ye hing, my cauldrife frien',
Your blue neb owre the lowe,
A snawy nichtcap may be seen
Upon Benarty's pow;
An' snaw upon the auld gean stump,
Wha's frostit branches hang
Oot owre the dyke abune the pump
That's gane clean aff the fang.
The pump that half the toun's folk ser'd,
It winna gie a jaw,
An' rouch, I ken, sall be your beard,
Until there comes a thaw.

Come, reenge the ribs, an' let the heat
Doon to oor tinglin' taes;
Clap on a guid Kinaskit peat
An' let us see a blaze;
An' since o' water we are scant,
Fess ben the barley-bree -
A nebfu' baith we sanna want
To wet oor whistles wi'!
Noo let the winds o' Winter blaw
Owre Scotland's hills and plains,
It maitters nocht to us ava -
We've simmer in oor veins!

The pooers o' Nature, wind and snaw,
Are far abune oor fit,
But while we scoog them, let them blaw;
We'll aye hae simmer yet.
An' sae wi' Fortune's blasts, my frien', -
They'll come an' bide at will,
But we can jink ahint a screen
An' jouk their fury still.
Then happy ilka day that comes,
An' glorious ilka nicht;
The present disna fash our thoombs,
The future needna fricht!

The warm glow that whisky gives makes it the perfect anti-dote to the snell, harsh weather of the Scottish winter, and all those sniffles, rheumatic aches and feelings of despair and depression that come with it. Countries get the drink their weather demands. No wonder Scotland's national drink is a golden glow giving inner warmth. This poem delivers a wonderfully snug and cosy interior contrasting with the inclement weather outside - a typical Scottish scene.

Neil Gow's Fareweel to Whisky

AGNES LYON 1762-1840

Ye've surely heard o famous Neil,
The man that played the fiddle weel;
I wat he was a canty chiel.
  An' dearly lo'ed the whisky, O.
An' aye sin he wore tartan hose,
He dearly lo'ed the Athole Brose;
An' wae was he, you may suppose,
  To bid fareweel to whisky, O.

Alake, quo' Neil, I'm frail an' auld,
And find my bluid grows unco cauld,
I think it maks me blythe and bauld,
  A wee drop Highland whisky, O.
But a' the doctors do agree
That whisky's no the drink for me;
I'm fley'd they'll gar me tyne my glee,
  Should they part me and whisky, O.

But I should mind on 'auld lang syne',
How paradise our friends did tyne,
Because something ran in their min' -
  Forbid, like Highland whisky, O.
While I can get both wine and ale,
And find my head and fingers hale,
I'll be content, though legs should fail,
  And though forbidden whisky, O.

I'll tak my fiddle in my hand,
And screw the strings up while they stand,
And mak a lamentation grand
  For guid auld Highland whisky, O.
O! a' ye pow'rs o music, come.
I find my heart grows unco glum;
My fiddlestrings will hardly bum
  To say, 'Fareweel to whisky, O'.

This song was written to the very popular fiddle tune 'Farewell to Whisky' written by one of Scotland's great composers, Neil Gow, who lived at Inver, near Dunkeld, at the end of the eighteenth century.

The song seems to suggest that while he believed whisky made him 'blythe and bauld', the doctor had other ideas. As Gow composed a later tune called 'Whisky Welcome Back Again', it seems he was able to get a second opinion. He outlived two wives and two of his sons, so it must have been good for him!

Actually, it is much more likely that the tune titles were chosen as comments on the law making the private distilling of whisky illegal and that Agnes Lyon's song lyric is a bit of an embellishment.

A Cogie o' Yill

ANDREW SHERIFFS (or SHERREFS) (1762-1800)

A cogie o' yill, and a pickle ait meal,
And a dainty wee drappie o' whisky,
Was our forefathers' dose, to sweel doon
    their brose,
And keep them aye cheerie and frisky.

Then hey for the whisky, and hey for the meal,
And hey for the cogie, an hey for the yill;
Gin ye steer a' thegither, they'll dae unco weel
To haud the heart cheerie and brisk aye.

When I see our Scots lads, wi' their kilts and
    cockauds,
That sae aften ha'e lounder'd our foes,
    man,
I think to mysel' on the meal and the yill,
And the fruits o' our Scottish kail brose,
    man.

Then hey for the whisky, &c.

When our brave Hieland blades, wi' their
    claymores and plaids,
In the field drive like sheep on our foes,
    man;
Their courage and power spring frae this to
    be sure -
They're the noble effects o' the brose, man.

Then hey for the whisky, &c.

But your spindle-shank'd sparks, wha sae ill
    fill their sarks;
Your pale-visaged milksops and beaux,
    man;
I think when I see them 'twere kindness to
    gi'e them
A cogie o' yill, or o' brose, man.

Then hey for the whisky, &c.

What John Bull despises our better sense
    prizes;
He denies eatin' blanter ava, man;
Tho' by eatin' o' blanter, his mare's grown,
    I'll w'rant her,
The nobler brute o' the twa, man.

Then hey for the whisky, &c.

The legendary strength and courage of Highland fighting men is here attributed to their diet of ale, whisky and oats. That may well be true, and I know from experience that whisky on your porridge sets you up for the day, but I'm not sure about mixing all three together!

The last verse has a dig at the English, who are known to be contemptuous of oats, asserting that the Scots staple should be fed to horses, not humans.

The author was a contemporary of Burns and was described by him as 'a little decrepid body, with some abilities'.

The Auld Doctor

DAVID RORIE (1867-1946)

O' a' the jobs that sweat the sark
Gie me the kintra doctor's wark,
Ye ca' awa, frae dawn till dark,
 Whate'er the weather be, O!

Some tinkler wife is in the strae,
Your boots are owre the taps wi' clay
Through wadin' bog an' sklimmin' brae
 The besom for to see, O!

Ye ken auld Jock o' Windybarns?
The bull had near ca'd oot his harns,
His een were blinkin' fu' o' starns,
 An' doon they ran for me, O!

There's ae guid wife, we're weel acquaint,
Nae trouble's kent but what she's taen't,
Yet aye she finds some new complaint,
 O' which I hae the key, O!

She's had some unco queer mishaps,
Wi' nervish wind and clean collapse,
An' naethin' does her guid but draps -
 Guid draps o' barley-bree, O!

I wouldna care a docken blade,
Gin her acoont she ever paid,
But while she gi'es me a' her trade,
 There's ne'er a word o' fee, O!

Then De'il hae a' thae girnin' wives,
There's ne'er a bairn they hae that thrives,
It's aye the kink-hoast or the hives
  That's gaun to gar them dee, O!

Tak' ony job ye like ava!
Tak' trade, the poopit or the law,
But gin ye're wise ye'll haud awa'
  Frae medical degree, O!

Another couple of afflictions helped by whisky - 'nervish wind and clean collapse'. It sounds like it's a cure for hypochondria too. I'm ever more convinced it should be made available on the NHS!

Ayrshire Jock

JOHN DAVIDSON (1857-1909)

I, John Auld, in my garret here,
In Sauchiehall Street, Glasgow, write,
Or scribble, for my writing-gear
Is sadly worn; a dirty white
My ink is watered to; and quite
Splay-footed is my pen - the handle
Bitten into a brush; my light,
Half of a ha'penny tallow-candle.

A little fire is in the grate,
Between the dusty bars, all red -
All black above; the proper state
To last until I go to bed.
I have a night-cap on my head,
And one smokes in a tumbler by me:
Since heart and brain are nearly dead,
Who would these comforters deny me?

Ghosts lurk about the glimmering room,
And scarce-heard whispers hoarsely fall:
I fear no more the rustling gloom,
Nor shadows moving on the wall;
For I have met at church and stall,
In streets and roads, in graveyards dreary,
The quick and dead, and know them all:
Nor sight nor sound can make me eerie.

Midnight rang out an hour ago;
Gone is the traffic in the street,
Or deadened by the cloak of snow
The gallant north casts at the feet
Of Christmas, as is meet;
With icicles the gutter bristles;
The wind that blows now slack, now fleet,
In every muffled chimney whistles.

I'll draw the blind and shut - alas!
No shutters here! . . . My waning sight
Sees through the naked window pass
A vision. Far within the night
A rough-cast cottage, creamy white,
With drooping eaves that need no gutters,
Flashes its bronze thatch in the light,
And flaps its old-style, sea-green shutters.

There I was born . . . I'll turn my back;
I would not see my boyhood days:
When later scenes my memory track,
Into the magic pane I'll gaze.
Hillo! The genial film of haze
Is globed and streaming on my tumbler:
It's getting cold; but this I'll praise,
Though I'm a universal grumbler.

Now, here's a health to rich and poor,
To lords and to the common flock,
To priests, and prigs, and - to be sure! -
Drink to yourself, old Ayrshire Jock;
And here's to rhyme, my stock and rock;
And though you've played me many a plisky,
And had me in the prisoners dock,
Here's my respects t'ye, Scottish whisky!

That's good! To get this golden juice
I starve myself and go threadbare.
What matter though my life be loose?
Few know me now, and fewer care.
Like many another lad from Ayr -
This is a fact, and all may know it -
And many a Scotchman everywhere,
Whisky and Burns made me a poet.

Just as the penny dreadfuls make
The 'prentice rob his masters till,
Ploughboys their honest work forsake,
Inspired by Robert Burns, They swill
Whisky like him, and rhyme; but still
Success attends on imitation
Of faults alone: to drink a gill
Is easier than to stir a nation.

They drink, and write their senseless
rhymes,
Tagged echoes of the lad of Kyle,
In mongrel Scotch: didactic times
In Englishing our Scottish style
Have yet but scotched it: in a while
Our bonny dialects may fade hence:
And who will dare to coin a smile
At those who grieve for their decadence?

These rhymesters end in scavenging,
Or carrying coals, or breaking stones;
But I am of a stronger wing,
And never racked my brains or bones.
I rhymed in English, catching tones
From Shelley and his great successors;
Then in reply to written groans,
There came kind letters from professors.

With these, and names of lords as well,
My patrons, I brought out my book;
And - here's my secret - sold, and sell
The same from door to door. I look
My age; and yet, since I forsook
Ploughing for poetry, my income
Comes from my book, by hook or crook;
So I have found the muses winsome.

That last rhyme's bad, the pun is worse;
But still the fact remains the same:
My book puts money in my purse,
Although it never brought me fame.
I once desired to make a name,
But hawking daily an edition
Of one's own poetry would tame
The very loftiest ambition.

Ah! Here's my magic looking glass!
Against the panes night visions throng.
Lo! There again I see it pass,
My boyhood! Ugh! The kettle's song
Is pleasanter, so I'll prolong
The night an hour yet. Soul and body!
There's surely nothing very wrong
In one more glass of whisky toddy!

An old poet looks back over his life – and what provides the perfect stimulus for some reminiscence therapy? Whisky! Old Jock describes it as his comforter. Is that not what they give infants in America? Could be something in it.

Come all ye
Jolly Hireman Lads

TALL STORIES AND MYTHICAL TALES

Scotland is a land with a fascinating history and a strong tradition of telling and re-telling stories. The folk song tradition in particular is full of story songs, from the oldest ballads to the bothy songs and contemporary writing. Young men and women will always have adventures, but strong drink, which loosens inhibitions, will tend to make those adventures more remarkable - not necessarily better or worse - but more remarkable.

The world of whisky, of course, has its own rich lore and many larger than life characters step from the pages of the industry's history book - the pioneers, the whisky barons, the smugglers; George Smith of Glenlivet who, as the first licensed distiller, was obliged to carry a pair of hair-trigger pistols to defend himself from antagonistic smugglers; Duncan Forbes of Culloden whose distillery at Ferintosh was exempt from paying duty for nearly a hundred years, basically because of his political allegiances; James Buchanan who hired unemployed actors to help him in unorthodox methods to promote his whisky in London. There is plenty of material waiting for today's poets and songwriters. However, it tends not to be the real characters that inhabit the songs and poems, but rather anonymous, slightly obscure, if not mythical folk from the fevered imaginations of the bardic fraternity. The stories and jokes we tell are similar - like the quintessential highlander who kept his promise to a life-long friend to pour his favourite whisky over his grave when he died. He just chose to filter it through his own body first.

Some of the mythical stories in this section are of biblical scenes, retold in our own Scots language and with our dry Scots sense of humour superimposed. Is this blasphemy or art?

The animal stories have a totemic feeling about them - some are undoubtedly anthropomorphic, with animals assuming the traits and behaviours of humans. In real life, it is much more likely that humans take on the nature of animals when drink is near. There was a local drinker in the Arisaig Hotel (the place where I first discovered malt whisky) whose nickname was Seagull, because whenever tourists came in to the bar he would head over and sit beside them hoping for free drink.

The Tarves Ramble

TRADITIONAL

Come all ye jolly hireman lads
And listen unto me
Ill tell to you a story
That's nae a word o' lee.
Wi a airy airrity aidie, aide
Airy airrity ann.

My name I needna mention
It's hardly worth the while
I am a jolly baillie lad
Near Tarves I do dwell.

I canna work your horses
I canna haud the plough
Cut nor build the harvest
But I can feed the coo.

It happened on an evening
To Tarves we did go
To get a dram and hae some fun
The truth I'll let you know.

When we arrived at Tarves
To Duthie's we did pad
And there we got some music
Which made our hearts right glad.

The chap that gave the music
His name I needna hide
He is a jolly ploughman lad
His name is Ironside.

Some was there for boots and shoes
And some was there for clothes
But he was there for treacle
He being on his brose.

Few was there that I did know
And as few there knew me
But there was one amongst the rest
That tried to bully me.

We next to Mr. Philip's went
To try and get some fun
There I was sore ensnared
Wi' the maiden of the inn.

She was a lovely maiden
If maiden that she be
Twa rosy cheeks, twa rollin' e'en
And a lovely girl was she.

We sat and drank and merry were
We drank I think na shame
When eleven o'clock began to strike
We steered our course for hame.

It was there I lost my comrade
And on him I did cry
Just at that very moment
A man in blue came by.

And he did plainly tell me
If I didna hold my tongue
He would take me into custody
Before that it was long.

He tried to drag me to the inn
His strength he didna spare
But I did plainly show to him
That he would need a pair.

But surely I am a profligate
A villain at the bone
To tear the coat from off his back
It being not his own.

But assistance soon unto him came
They dragged me to the door
There I was made a prisoner
And left to think it o'er.

A sudden thought came in my mind
I up the window drew
Twa willing hands did pull me out
That didna like the blue.

I think the folk in Tarves
A jail would need to get
For to lock up their prisoners
And nae let them escape.

For surely it maun be a sin
To break the Sabbath day
Searching for their prisoners
When they do run away.

I've something more to tell you
Which adds to my disgrace
To Aberdeen I was brought up
Just for to plead my case.

The judge in passing sentence
I heard it like a shot
There was thirty shillings to pay down
And fifteen for the coat.

Now all ye jolly hireman lads
A warning take by me
When you go down to Tarves
Pray don't get on the spree.

But get what you are wanting
And steer your course for hame
And when a row it does break up
You winna get the blame.

This is a typical bothy ballad, telling of the adventures of a spree. I would say there is a very good chance it is basically a true story. The baillie lads tended the cattle and were lower in the ferm-toun pecking order than ploughmen and even than the orra loons. They were the ones who had to get up earliest – sometimes 4.00am – to see to the milking, so being out on a spree could be a rare occasion.

Ironically, when the 20th century brought the tractor, it was the ploughmen who gradually became obsolete, while the role of the baillie was safe.

The Greig-Duncan collection has tunes for some variants of the Tarver Ramble or the Tarves Rant, but I have not been able to find a tune for this version.

The Queer Folk i' the Shaws

JAMES FISHER (1818-?)

I thocht unto mysel' ae day I'd like to see a Race,
For mony ither lads like me had been to sic a place;
Sae up I gat an' was'd mysel', put on my Sunday braws,
An' wi' a stick into my hand I started for the Shaws!

My mither tichtly coonsell'd me before that I gaed oot,
To tak' gude care and mind my e'e wi' what I was aboot;
Said she 'Ye may be trod to death beneath the horses' paws;
An' mind ye, lad, the sayin's true – 'There's queer folk i' the Shaws!' '

The races pleased me unco weel – gosh! They were grand to see:
The horses ran sae awfu' swift, I thocht they maist did flee;
When they cam' near the winnin'-post – O, siccan loud huzzas!
Ye wad hae thocht they'd a' gane daft – the queer folk i' the Shaws!

A bonnie lass cam' up to me and asked me for a gill;
Quoth I, 'If that's the fashion here, I mauna tak' it ill.'
She wiled me owre intil a tent, an' half-a-mutchkin ca's;
Thinks I, my lass, I see it's true – There's queer folk i' the Shaws!

The whisky made my love to bleeze, I fand in perfect bliss,
So I gripp'd the lassie roun' the neck to tak' a wee bit kiss;
When in a crack she lifts her neive and bangs it in my jaws;
Says I, 'My dear, what means a' this? – There's queer folk i' the Shaws!'

A strappin' chiel cam' forrit then and took awa' my lass,
Misca'd me for a kintra clown - a stupid silly ass;
Says I, 'If I've dune ony ill juist lat me ken the cause' -
He made his fit spin aff my hip - There's queer folk i' the Shaws!

Aroused at last, I drew my fist, and gied him on the lug,
Though sairly I was worried for't by his big collie dug;
It bit my legs, it bit my airms, it tore my Sunday braws,
And in the row I lost my watch, wi' the queer folk i' the Shaws.

The police then cam' up to me, and hauled me aff to quod;
They put their twines aboot my wrists, and thump'd me on the road;
They gar'd me pay a gude poundnote ere I got oot their claws;
Catch me again when I'm ta'en in by the queer folk i' the Shaws.

The 'Shaws' referred to is Pollockshaws in Glasgow. Pollock estate was the setting for a well-known annual horse race. There are lots of songs in which the slightly naive country boy is taken advantage of by the more street-wise city folk. Any song in which horses have paws and policemen have claws is guaranteed to have an element of charm.

Alan MacLean

TRADITIONAL

I was born in Cullen,
A minister's son,
Brocht up wi' guid learnin'
Till my school days were done.

I went to the college
A student to be,
But the marriage at Westfield
Has quite ruined me.

There was Grant and Mackenzie,
Macdonald and I,
And we went to the weddin'
Pretty girls for to spy.

We danced and we sang
And we took great delight,
And bonnie Sally Allan
Cam oft in my sight.

'O Sally, dear Sally,
Will you take a dram?'
'O yes, my dear Alan,
If it comes from your hand.'

I gied her a dance
And I gied her a dram,
And I asked her quite kindly
If she'd go to the broom.

She disliked my offer
But gave the least froon.
Says she, 'My dear Alan,
Had it been my doom.'

So we went to the broom
In the middle o' the night;
We had neither coal nor candle
But the moon gave us light.

But her father next morning
To the College he came;
He was all in a passion
At Alan MacLean.

'If it's true.' Says the Regent,
'As I fear it's no lie,
This day from Aulton College
Young Alan must fly.'

'Tomorrow's the graduation
And Tuesday's the Ball,
But well banish young Alan
From the Aulton College Hall.'

My father's a minister,
He preaches at Tain.
My mother died in the Hielands
And I durna gang hame.

It's I intended a minister
But that winna do;
It's now for a doctor
That I maun pursue.

Prince Charles the Royal
Lies out in the bay,
Takin' on goods and passengers
And she'll surely take me.

Fare ye weel, Aulton College,
Likewise Aberdeen.
Fare ye weel, Sally Allan,
Who lives by yon green.

If ever I return again
As I hope that I shall,
We shall have a merry bottle
Near the Aulton College Hall.

A slightly sad and cautionary tale of how a young woman, under the influence of whisky, might do things she otherwise wouldn't. It must be said that, for all his ruination and sorry plight, young Allan seems, from the last verse, to have a bit of resilience in him.

I like the comment that since the scandal has made it impossible for him to become a minister, he'll have to make do with becoming a doctor!

Jock Geddes and the Soo

TRADITIONAL

Jock Geddes on some business bent
Tae mairket yin day gaed licht-hairtit:
His mither, carefu o' her son,
Saw Jock fu-trig ere he depairtit.
Noo Jock at mairket whiles got fou
A place where wily scamps wad trick him –
And so his mither at the door cries,
'Come hame sober, Jock, ye nickum!'

Braw, braw tae be weel-likit
Braw, braw tae be sae bonnie:
Braw says Jock, it is tae be
Sae muckle thocht on by sae mony.

But Jock as usual soon forgot
The plain injunctions o' his mither:
The mairket made him awfa dry –
The cure was whisky, deil anither!
He met a freen as dry's himsel
And aff they went tae weet their wizens:
Gless efter gless gaed doon until
The total number cam tae dizens.

Braw, braw, &c.

Jock rase at last and made for hame:
He hadnae taen his mither's biddin:
He couldna thrive - he tripped an fell
Wi a' his length across the midden.
Jock jist lay still, fell fast asleep:
The drink had fairly stopped his kickin,
The soo came by and smelt his moo,
And likin' that commenced the lickin'!

Braw, braw, &c.

The curious soo still lickit on:
Cries Jock, 'Noo Jean, haud aff, that's plenty!
Let Kirsty hae a smack or twa,
A'm sure that ye've had mair than twenty!
I ken I am a weel-faur'd chiel
But dinna get in sic a swither
I'll let ye kiss me, but God's sake
Ye needna eat me a' thegither'.

Braw, braw, &c.

At last his sober sense came roon
An' lookin up saw Sandy Cam'ell:
'Ye muckle, nasty, ugly brute,
Nae mair upon me will ye wammle!'
Jock rase an spat for near an oor:
The soo had played an awfu plisky!
The brute was killed the very next day,
And Jock has niver since taen whisky.

Braw, braw, tae be weel-likit,
Braw, braw it is but bless me,
Owre weel-likit winna dae –
Ah niver thocht a soo wad kiss me!

Do animals like whisky?
According to this song they do.
*   It appears that the original*
source of this song may have
been a competition in 'The
Peoples Friend'.
*   Note the inevitable disap-*
proval and misfortune that is
the fate in Scotland of all who
over-indulge in drams.

The Gulls o' Invergordon

TRADITIONAL

In Invergordon by the sea they built a great
    distillery,
And every gull is on a spree that lives in
    Invergordon-O.
The mash that's flowin from the still they
    gobble doon wi right guid will
And every gull can haud his gill that lives in
    Invergordon-O.

Dirra ma do a dram a day
Dirra ma do ma daddy-O
Dirra ma do a dram a day
The gulls o' Invergordon-O.

A Glesca gull came fae the Clyde in
    Invergordon fur tae bide,
He found himself half stupified wi the gulls
    o' Invergordon-O
And then he found to his surprise that he
    was hardly fit tae rise
And flyin a sort o' side-i-weys as he left
    Invergordon-O.

Dirra ma do, &c.

And when we die, some people say; we come back in some other way.
O how I'd love to come and stay as a gull in Invergordon-O.
O dirra ma do a dram a day - reincarnation would be gay,
A sort o' perpetual Hogmanay as a gull in Invergordon-O.

Dirra ma do, &c.

Yet more evidence that animals are partial to a wee drop. I got this song from Colin MacAllister, who says it was widely sung in the North East of Scotland during the 1960s. Colin has a wealth of Irish whisky songs, but then that's another project altogether.

Smokey the Cat

ROBIN LAING

Smokey the cat came from nowhere;
Just whisped in under some door;
Sniffed quietly around
And knew that she'd found
The best place to stay in Bowmore.

She'd arrived at Bowmore distillery
Where the finest malt whisky is made.
There was no welcome mat
For Smokey the cat
But she liked the place - so she stayed.

They say cats have more than one life
With re-incarnation and that.
Whether it's true
All that cat deja vu,
Smokey's a born again cat.

There's something about her that takes you
Back to the Lords of the Isles
When the cats of Finlaggan
Would go scallywaggin'
For miles and miles and miles.

It's the way she melts into the shadows
Or suddenly creeps up on folk
She'll always find you
Slinking behind you
The cat who was named after smoke.

She sits on the sill of the maltings
On days when the weather is nice
And while one eye sleeps
The other one keeps
A lookout for small birds and mice.

Small birds and mice eat the barley
So Smokey confronts them foursquare
But she pulls in her claws
And quietly ignores
The Angels who come for their share.

Felines don't care for whisky
Everyone understands that
But that peaty odour
Beneath the pagoda
Owes something to Smokey the cat.

On Islay people made whisky
Long before it was chic.
The cat from Bowmore
Is nothing more
Than the ghost of the island's peat-reek.

Islay is a great place to spend a few days. It has lovely old Celtic stone crosses, long beaches, fresh lobster, farmed oysters and eight distilleries.

The hub of the island is the main town of Bowmore. The main street has the famous round church of Bowmore at the top and the distillery at the bottom. The church was built in its unusual round shape so that the devil would find no corners to hide in. Why he would waste his time in the church, when there is a distillery at the other end of the street, I don't know.

When I visited the distillery in 1998, the devil was not in evidence, but there were plenty of angels and a cat. I was introduced to Smokey and penned this little piece for her.

Cats are a bit of a theme in distillery life with perhaps the most famous, being Towser at Glenturret distillery. Towser was in the Guinness Book of Records for having caught the greatest ever number of mice – 28,899! I wonder who was counting.

Then there was the poor little cat who stowed away in a shipment of bourbon barrels from Kentucky. When she arrived in Keith four weeks later, she was half-starved and out of her head on whisky fumes. The staff at Chivas Brothers adopted the cat and had it quarantined. Once it had been sobered up and fed, it found its new name was Dizzy.

The Ghost Wi' the Squeaky Wheel

TOM CLELLAND

Now Wullie was a fearless man.
While other fellows turned and ran,
He'd shake the shiver from his hands
And stand up straight and weel.
All superstitions he disdained
As spooky stories fit for weans
Till he met a phantom of his ain,
A ghost wi' a squeaky wheel.

The bells had claimed the Old Year end
And Wullie gone first-footing friends
Then, blithely, turning home again
He took the river road.
The moon was full with frosty bite,
The water deep and still and iced,
His breath like silver stars at night,
No living soul abroad.

Now blended whisky's power is slight
Guid malt could face the deil,
Should you meet on a winter's night
A ghost wi' a squeaky wheel.

Past Crossford park and village sign,
The iron brig and wall behind,
The Silver Birch and old hedge line,
Wull sauntered worry-free,
When in the distance came a grate –
A sound that made him stand and wait,
Like the swinging of some hellish gate
A rasping, rhythmic gree.

Wull stood transfixed as it drew near.
The squeaking growing ever clear.
A piercing echo through his ears,
From the depths of hell it rang
And a sight that gripped him to the marrow.
A figure, ghostly grey and hollow,
A grisly shape that pushed a barrow
With the face of old Boab Lang.

Now blended whisky's, &c.

'Well Boab', says Wull, and showed no fear
'It's unco strange tae see you here.
We havenae crossed these twenty years
And mony's an Auld Lang Syne.'
The ghost looked Wullie in the eye
And, in a mournful voice, did cry
'Beware poor sinner, born to die
Be ready for your time.

We all maun pass, each single yin,
Our earthly pockets filled wi' sin,
That drags us doon and draws us in
To this world and its sorrows.
Damned selfishness that breeds despair,
Transgressions, greedy, cruel and sair
We a' hae sins but I had mair –
Enough to fill this barrow.'

Now blended whisky's, &c.

'The Clyde, the burn and Nethan River
Will bind me on this road forever
Running water I can never
Cross nor bridges breach.'
'Tween these three points, traverse I must.
These chains and torture serve me just
But the worst is this infernal rust
And this old wheel's hellish screech.'

Says Wull, 'My freen, I cannae judge –
I'll try help you with your drudge'
But the barrow Wullie couldnae budge
Like it was solid steel.
'I have the very dab' cries he
'The finest whisky's all you need'
His good malt Wullie freely gied
and poured it on the wheel.

The whisky stopped the squeaking dead.
The echo ceased in Wullie's head.
The ghostly figure smiled instead
And silence once more reigned.
Wull crossed the bridge at Hazel burn
His good deed done, his sleep well earned.
He watched Auld Boab as he did turn
and start back down again.

Now blended whisky's, &c.

CODA
Ah listen sinners – and take heed
Beware life's cruel, deceitful deeds.
To ease the tortures of a hell,
Remember Auld Boab's barrow well
A good spirit is all you really need

*This song is loosely based on a story, told to
Tom Clelland by the late Wull Baxter, about a
ghost who walks the road between Crossford
and Hazelbank , pushing a barrow with a
squeaky wheel. You hear him before you see
him. And whisky is a good thing to have in your
workshop too.*

The Best O' the Barley

BRIAN McNEILL

My uncle Jim served his time
On the shores of the Forth as a joiner
And three pounds ten a week was all he
earned.
But the wages were better working Michigan
pine
So he sailed on an ocean liner
To build a better life with the trade he'd
learned.

And the shore he reached in '23,
The home of the brave and the land of the
free,
Was as dry as the Devil's tongue on judge-
ment day.
But to find a dram in a foreign land
Is the natural gift of a Falkirk man
And Lady Liberty looked the other way.
Or so I've always heard my uncle say.

He's the best of the barley, cream of the crop.
Go easy on the water and I'll tell you when to stop.
Would you please charge your glasses with the pure,
clear drop
And drink to the best o' the barley.

My uncle Jim was a child of his time
And the tricks of the time they were dirty.
And the dirtiest of all was the one they
played
On a working man's dollar and the poor
man's dime between '29 and '30
For they killed all the steady jobs in the
building trade.

And the only way that Jim could see
Was to play the game with Lady Liberty
Though no-one ever told him all the rules.
And when fainter hearts were homeward
bound
Jim sold Michigan ice by the pound
With a leather sling and an iron hook for
tools.
Just to show the Yankees how to keep their
cool.

He's the best of the barley, &c.

My uncle Jim he could keep good time
When the band played an eightsome reel
And he loved to waltz away the summer
    nights.
And the spring in his step kept him in his
    prime
Through the turns of fortune's wheel
And it spun him through the darkness and
    the light.

And to dance the jig of history
Jim took the hand of the century
And never let her steal a backward glance.
From the D-Day beaches to the cold lake
    shore
He whirled her round and round the floor
To show her how a Scotsman takes his
    chance
And he never missed a measure of the
    dance.

He's the best of the barley, cream of the crop.
Go easy on the water and I'll tell you when to stop.
Would you please charge your glasses with the pure,
    clear drop
And drink to the best o' the barley,
To Scotland and the Best O' the Barley

This song is from Brian McNeill's album 'The Back o' the North Wind' which is on the theme of Scots who have moved to America. It has a strong tune and a great 'whisky' chorus. It makes reference to the period of Prohibition in the USA, a time which had a significant impact on the development of the Scotch whisky industry. Many Scots were involved in running illegal whisky into the States, up and down the Eastern seaboard and over the Canadian border. Michigan would undoubtedly have been one of the entry points. Indeed one of the Beaver Island archipelago group in the north of Lake Michigan is called Whiskey Island to this day.

Three Men Frae Overtoon

BILLY STEWART

There were three men frae Overtoon were
   travelling hame yin nicht;
While waiting for a ferry boat they spied
   and awfy fecht,
For workers frae the Garrion Brig had set
   upon the toon
And the village people o' Dalserf were try-
   ing tae put them doon.

And they fought in the streets o' Dalserf toon
Past every But and Ben
But it took three men frae Overtoon
Tae bring it tae an end.

And when the men frae Overtoon they saw
   this dreadful scene
They thought the only thing to do was they
   should intervene
And so they told the villagers 'Look these
   are desperate men'
And they stopped the marchers frae the
   Brig and sent them back again.

And they fought, &c.

The villagers cried oot wi' delight, Dalserf it
   had been saved
And to the men frae Overtoon a gift to
   them they gave;
Six gallons o' fine whisky, yes that would be
   their own,
But they would not be given any cask to take
   it home.

And they fought, &c.

Well at this very crafty ploy the villagers did
   hoot,
Until the men frae Overtoon had each
   ta'en aff his boots
The boots were tied thegither, roon' the
   horses' necks were slung,
Then the men frae Overtoon said the
   whisky should be brung.

And they fought, &c.

A gallon of the whisky fitted nicely in each
  buit;
When the villagers they saw this, well they
  nearly had a fit.
They knew that they'd been bested and they
  loudly heaved a sigh
As in their stocking soles the three men
  bade them all good-bye.

And they fought, &c.

And so the men frae Overtoon they
  climbed the Horsley brae
And the whisky seemed to make the men
  and horses slightly sway
And all the folk fare Overtoon came oot tae
  see the sicht
Wi six gallons o the whisky well they had a
  rare guid nicht.

And they fought, &c.

The song was based on a poem 'The Riot Of Dalserf' by Thomas B. Kerr. Dalserf village had developed round an important crossing point on the Clyde and the building of Garrion Bridge, in 1817, was a threat to its prosperity. That is the background to the riot referred to in the song. Certainly the population of Dalserf shrank from 1100 in 1775 to 112 in 1841. This may have had a lot to do with the closure of local mines, but the new bridge would have been a major factor.
Billy Stewart lives in Overtown and he tells me that the locals still have a reputation for getting involved in other people's fights and drinking whisky out of sweaty boots.

The Devil Uisge Beatha

ALAN REID

He watches for the gauger man that prowls
the countyside,
He hides his liquid treasure then waits for
night and rides
Ower the Torrance burn tae Glesca where
there's plenty that will buy her,
She's that sweet forbidden devil uisge beatha.

Whisky is a devil jaud that burns the brains o' man,
He'll dance or stagger, sing or fight,
He'll argue black and blue is white.
The fermer's wife, the weeda and the weary workin'
man,
They fill the air wi' curses on that devil uisge beatha.

A band o' wild marauders in the colours o'
Colquhoun
Were camped among the Campsie moors
above the Lennoxtoon.
The folk below were soon tae know they
were Clan Gregor men
When they came sweepin' doon the
Campsie Glen.

They scattered a' before them, a' the
weemin and the bairns,
They chased the fermin' workers and the
fermers frae their hames,
They gethered up the cattle and they
camped aside the hill
And there they fund the hidden whisky still.

Whisky is a devil jaud, &c.

The Campsie men assembled then tae see
what could be done
But shepherd lads and cottars cannae match
a hielan' band.
They cursed the theivin' reivers and their
heathen heilan' cries
As they drank their fill aneath the evenin'
skies.

Whisky is a devil jaud, &c.

Whisky is the devil jaud that burns the
   brains o' men
For in the night the heilan' men fell drunk
   upon the grun'.
The Campsie men crept up to them and
   slew them as they lay
And a' was back in order by the day.

There's stills above the clachan, there's still
   aroon' the fells
There's stills aroon' the countryside nae
   gauger man can smell.
But the one that snared the Gregor was
   mair valuable than ten
Tae the honest fermers o' the Campsie
   Glen.

Whisky is a devil jaud that burns the brains o' man,
He'll dance or stagger, sing or fight,
He'll argue black and blue is white.
The fermer's wife, the weeda and the weary workin'
   man,
They fill the air wi' blessin's on that devil uisge beatha.

Alan Reid, founder member of
Battlefield Band, found this
apparently true story in a book
about the local history of the
area he lives in. There was a
time when those who lived on
the fringes of the highlands had
as much trouble from maraud-
ing Highlanders as the
Borderers had from reivers on
either side. The MacGregors
were a particularly trouble-
some bunch, so much so that
they were outlawed and even
the name was proscribed.
   Ever since the poor Cyclops
got blind drunk in the Odyssey,
the idea of the bad guys
becoming vulnerable through
getting pissed has been a popu-
lar one. The song bridges us
nicely into the next section.

The Wedding at Cana –
or water intae uisge beatha

JAMES S. ADAM

The kintraside fae miles aroon
    tae Cana cam tae see them wad,
The Lord, his mither, honoured guests,
    an a' the twal as weel were bade.

The fiddlers elbows jinked and jouked,
    twa boxes swalled the lichtsome tune;
A scene o' fun and jollity,
    as dancers and big drams birled roon.

But in the midst of life comes daith,
    oor dearest pleasures we maun tine;
Like crack o' doom the message rang,
    Oh, Son, they've clean rin oot o' wine.

That joab has nocht tae dae wi' me,
    guidwife, an even less wi you;
We baith ken fine ma time's no come,
    sae, wumman, dinna fash me noo.

His mither, no a tait abashed,
    gaed roon tae tell the sairvants ha',
Ma lad's a richt guid clever chiel
    Whate'er he bids, jist dae it a'.

The fear an tighe syne nearly grat
    (tae keep guests happy he maun try)
But whether fowk maun dee or wad,
    the deepest wells will aye rin dry.

It's a' thae sooks that gether roon,
    Ye'll hear their thirsty thrapples glock;
As sune's they ken the drams are free,
    nae bonded store that drouth could slock.

A fearsome gloom fell ower the room,
    as sairvants taomed the last wine goût;
The weemen thocht it juist as weel,
    disjaskit men mair dooncast grew.

The Lord took peety at the sicht,
    He coulda thole tae see fowk dowf,
For waddins should be gledsome times,
    an drooth maks aye a mirthless howff.

He ca'd the waiters roon aboot,
    Yon sax big muckle jars ower there,
Gae fill ilk ane richt tae its mou
    wi' watter – an wi naethin mair.

Oor auld guidman whae looks sae wae,
    can smooth thae wrunkles fae his broo;
Gey near two hunder gallons mair
    should surely see his waddin through.

Noo draw ye aff a richt guid dram
    for major domo here tae pree;
Afore ye serve mair drinks again,
    his pleasure maun be plain tae see.

But still an on, I'll no complain
     – wi a' that water intae wine;
Bring back the fiddlin, jigs and reels,
     this waddin noo will gang just fine.

The guests exalted late gaed hame,
     excited they'd the glimmer seen
O God's great wark an muckle poo'er
     writ firm in watter's shiftin sheen.

In that first marvel we perceive
     a lesson that content can bring;
God gave man watter an guid wine,
     that aye wi baith his hert micht sing.

The major domo sooked it doon,
     he licked and smacked his lips wi joy;
If guid plain watter made this dram,
     bring mair, and keep on poorin, boy.

But syne he cried the guidman ower,
     I hae a craw tae pick wi you;
Whit wey did ye no tell me first
     ye'd gotten sic a braw-like brew?

A wycelike man sterts wi his best,
     an syne when merry grows the room,
An when they've drunk an tined their blas,
     in cookin sherry they can soom.

But you, ye daft auld doited carle,
     ye couped the custom tapsalteer;
Wi' guests sae fou, ye muckle stot,
     your brawest wine is gey sma beer.

Here in Scotland we make a business of turning water into whisky, and there are those who would say that the process is indeed miraculous. But to be able to do it in the twinkling of an eye – well, who wouldn't worship the man who could do that.

The Deluge

W. D. COCKER (1882-1970)

The Lord took a staw at mankind,
A rightous an' natural scunner;
They were neither to haud nor to bind,
They were frichtit nae mair wi' his thun'er.

They had broken ilk edic' an' law,
They had pitten his saints to the sword,
They had worshipped fause idols o' stane;
'I will thole it nae mair', saith the Lord.

'I am weary wi' flytin' at folk;
I will dicht them clean oot frae my sicht;
But Noah, douce man, I will spare
For he ettles, puir chiel, to dae richt.'

So he cried unto Noah ae day,
When naebody else was aboot,
Sayin' 'Hearken, my servant, to Me
An' these, my commandments, cairry oot:

'A great, muckle boat ye maun build,
An ark that can float heich an' dry,
Wi' room in't for a' yer ain folk
An' a hantle o' cattle forby.

'Then tak' ye the fowls o' the air,
Even unto big bubbly-jocks;
An' tak' ye the beasts o' the field:
Whittrocks, an foumarts, an' brocks.

'Wale ye twa guid anes o' each,
See that nae cratur rebels;
Dinna ye fash aboot fish;
They can look efter theirsels.

'Herd them a' safely aboard,
An' ance the Blue Peter's unfurled,
I'll send doun a forty-day flood
And de'il tak' the rest o' the world.'

Sae Noah wrocht hard at the job,
An' searched to the earth's farthest borders,
An' gethered the beasts an' the birds
An' tell't them to staun' by for orders.

An' his sons, Ham an' Japheth an' Shem,
Were thrang a' this time at the wark;
They had felled a wheen trees in the wood
An' biggit a great, muckle ark.

This wisna dune juist on the quate,
An' neebours would whiles gether roon';
Then Noah would drap them a hint
Like: 'The weather is gaun to break doun.'

But the neebours wi' evil were blin'
An' little jaloused what was wrang,
Sayin': 'That'll be guid for the neeps,'
Or: 'The weather's been drouthy ower
  lang.'

Then Noah, wi' a' his ain folk,
An' the beasts an' the birds got aboard:
An' they steekit the door o' the ark,
An' they lippened theirsels to the Lord.

Then doun cam a lashin' o' rain,
Like the wattest wat day in Lochaber;
The hailstanes like plunkers cam' stot,
An' the fields turned to glaur, an' syne
  glabber.

An' the burns a' cam' doun in a spate,
An' the rivers ran clean ower the haughs,
An' the brigs were a' soopit awa',
An' what had been dubs becam' lochs.

Then the folk were sair pitten aboot,
An' they cried, as the weather got waur:
'Oh! Lord, we ken fine we hae sinn'd
But a joke can be carried ower faur!'

Then they chapp'd at the ark's muckle
    door,
To speer gin douce Noah had room;
But Noah ne'er heedit their cries,
He said: 'This'll learn ye to soom.'

An' the river roared loudly an' deep;
An' the miller was droon't in the mill;
An' the watter spread ower a' the land,
An' the shepherd was droon't on the hill.

But Noah, an' a' his ain folk,
Kep' safe frae the fate o' ill men,
Till the ark, when the flood had gi'en ower,
Cam' dunt on the tap o' a ben.

An' the watters row'd back to the seas,
An' the seas settled doun and were calm.
An' Noah replenished the earth –
But they're sayin' he took a guid dram!

OK – this is not really a whisky poem, but it is a beauty, and it paints on an enormous canvas
the familiar picture of a dram as the fitting reward for having completed a difficult task.

Oh, What a Parish

TRADITIONAL

Oh, what a parish, a terrible parish
Oh, what a parish is that o' Dunkel';
They hangit their minister, droon'd their precentor,
Dang doon the steeple and fuddled the bell.
The steeple was doon, but the kirk was still staun'in';
So they biggit a lum whaur the bell used tae hang.
A still-pot they got and they brewed Hieland whisky;
On Sundays they drank it and ranted and sang.

Oh, had ye but seen how gracefu' they lookit,
Crammed in the pews - socially joined.
MacDonald the piper struck up in the poopit.
He made the pipes skirl wi' music devine
When drink free'd their care they would curse and they'd swear;
They ranted and sang what they darena weel tell;
'Bout Geordie and Cherlie they bothered fu' rarely,
Wi' whisky they're worse than the Devil himsel'.

When the heart-cheerin' spirit had mounted their garrets,
Tae a ball on the green they a' did ajourn.
The maids in coats kilted then steppit and lilted;
When tired or dry tae the kirk they'd return.
If kirks a' owre Scotland held sic social meetings,
Nae warnin' they'd need frae a far-tinklin' bell,
For kindness and friendship would ca' them thegither,
Far better than roarin' the horrors o' Hell.

Oh, what a parish, a terrible parish.
Oh, what a parish is that o' Dunkel'.
They hangit their Minister, droon'd their Precentor,
Dang doon the steeple and fuddled the bell.
But let me advise ye that mischief there lies,
When neebours are drinkin wi' mair than themselves.
O' yer heart and yer hand try tae keep some command,
Or ye'll end up as bad as the folk o' Dunkel'

This is a real pastiche of an early tradi-
tional song with some verses added by
Adam Crawford, an Edinburgh tailor,
and some others by an unknown Glasgow
author. The tune, 'Over the Water to
Charlie' was married to the song by Andy
M. Stewart who has recorded a version on
his album 'By the Hush'.

The historic basis for the song seems to
lie in Kinkell, Strathearn, not Dunkeld,
and the facts have undoubtedly been
embellished in good folk tradition.
Nonetheless it is a perfect example in song
of the religious tensions that surround the
social history of whisky drinking.

Sanct Mungo

ALEXANDER RODGER (1784-1846)

Sanct Mungo wals ane famous sanct,
And ane cantye carle wals hee,
Hee drank o' ye Molendinar Burn,
Quhan bettere hee culdna prie;

Zit quhan hee culd gette strongere cheere,
Hee neuer wals wattere drye,
Bot drank o' ye streame o' ye wimpland
    worme,
And loot ye burne rynne bye.

Sanct Mungo wals ane merry sanct,
And merrylye hee sang;
Quhaneuer hee liltit uppe hys sprynge,
Ye very Firre Parke rang;

Both thoch hee weele culd lilt and synge,
And mak' sweet melodye,
Hee chauntit aye ye bauldest straynes,
Quhan prymed wi' barlye-bree.

Sanct Mungo wals ane godlye sanct,
Farre-famed for godlye deedis,
And grete delyte hee daylye took
Inn countand owre hys beadis;

Zit I, Sanct Mungo's youngeste sonne,
Can count als welle als hee;
Bot ye beadis quilk I like best to count
Are ye beadis o' barlye-bree.

Sanct Mungo wals ane jollie sanct:-
Sa weele hee lykit gude zil,
Thatte quhyles hee staynede hys quhyte
    vesture,
Wi' dribblands o' ye still;

Bot I, hys maist unwordye sonne,
Haue gane als farre als hee,
Far aince I tynd my garmente skirtis,
Throuch lufe o' barlye-bree.

*This piece was written around 1832. It is
written in an affected late mediaeval style,
because it is supposed to be the son of Saint
Mungo who is speaking. Saint Mungo is of
course the patron Saint of Glasgow and he
is slandered slightly in this. Alexander
Rodger was considered one of the Glasgow
poets of the time, although he was actually
born in East Calder.*

*The piece was originally set to music
and arranged as a glee for three voices.*

The De'il's Awa' Wi' th' Exciseman

TAXATION, SMUGGLING AND ILLICIT STILLS: THE WHISKY WARS

The Scots seem to be amazingly indifferent to the punishing levels of tax on their national drink. About two thirds of the cost of a bottle of whisky is tax. As whisky is subject to duty when it comes out of the bond and then suffers VAT on the full price, it is a commodity that is taxed twice. The high level of tax means that whisky is about half the price in many other European countries. This ought to be terribly painful to the Scots. If the French or the Spanish found their national drinks half the price in neighbouring countries there would be a revolt and direct action on a massive scale; ports would be blockaded, roads would come to a standstill, effigies of politicians would be soaked in alcohol and ceremonially burned and heads would roll.

But the Scots put up with it weakly, without a murmur. If we do complain it is always in a joke and there are a few examples of that in this book. Because we have such a deep psychological need to punish ourselves for enjoying whisky – tax actually has a useful, if twisted role to play.

Up to the early part of the eighteenth century ordinary people made whisky, mostly on a small scale, with very little interference from government. Throughout the eighteenth century, however a series of laws were passed by the London-based government, aimed either at increasing duty from whisky or restricting the unlicensed manufacture of the spirit. By the end of the century and into the first two decades of the nineteenth century, the situation that had developed was intolerably complicated, ineffective and unfair. Lowland distillers were only able to survive by making bad whisky, highland distillers were unable to sell their far superior product outside of their own areas, duty had been hiked up to unbearable levels to support the war against France (an old Scottish ally) and private or illicit stills were being hunted down ruthlessly. The age of smuggling had arrived.

This was a period when bands of smugglers were operating throughout Scotland to get the product of thousands of illicit stills to market. These smugglers were able to challenge the authority of the Excisemen or gaugers quite openly because they had the implicit support of the population. This was a notorious but colourful time in the history of whisky.

It was only in the 1820s and 30s that things began to improve after the landowners agreed to work against the smugglers if the government would rationalise the laws affecting legal distillers. It is from this time that the serious making of good quality whisky began to flourish. As the industry developed, the government enjoyed a steadily increasing rate of taxation. This rate was driven up particularly hard during the first and second world wars. Needless to say, rates driven up by war seldom come back down in peace-time.

The loss of the centuries-old right to make whisky, the days of the whisky wars against the excisemen, the ever-increasing taxation of our national drink and events like the wreck of the S. S. Politician have lodged in the folk memory and continue to stimulate the creative imagination of the Scots.

The Author's Earnest Cry And Prayer

To the Scotch representatives in the House of Commons

ROBERT BURNS (1759-1796)

Ye Irish lords, ye knights an' squires,
Wha represent our brughs an shires,
An' doucely manage our affairs
   In Parliament,
To you a simple poet's prayers
   Are humbly sent.

Alas! My roupit muse is hearse;
Your Honours' heart wi' grief 'twad pierce
To see her sitten on her arse
   Low i' the dust,
An' screechin' out poetic verse
   An' like to brust!

Tell them wha hae the chief direction,
Scotland an' me's in great affliction,
E'er sin' they laid that curst restriction
   On aqua vitae;
An' rouse them up to strong conviction,
   An' move their pity.

Stand forth, an' tell yon Premier youth
The honest, open, naked truth:
Tell him o' mine an' Scotland's drouth,
   His servants humble:
The muckle devil blaw ye south,
   If ye disemble!

Does ony great man glunch an' gloom?
Speak out, an' never fash your thumb!
Let posts an' pensions sink or soom
   Wi' them wha grant them;
If honestly they canna come,
   Far better want them.

In gath'rin' votes you were na slack;
Now stand as tightly by your tack;
Ne'er claw your lug, an' fidge your back,
   An' hum an' haw;
But raise your arm an' tell your crack
   Before them a'.

Paint Scotland greetin owre her thrissle;
Her mutchkin stoup as toom's a whissle:
An' damn'd Excisemen in a bussle,
   Seizin' a stell,
Triumphant crushin't like a mussle
   Or limpet shell.

Then on the tither hand present her,
A blackguard smuggler, right behint her,
An' cheek-for-chow, a chuffie vintner,
   Colleaguing join,
Pickin' her pouch as bare as Winter
   Of a' kind coin.

Is there that bears the name o' Scot,
But feels his heart's bluid rising hot,
To see his poor auld mither's pot
　　Thus dung in staves,
An' plundre'd o' her hindmost groat
　　By gallows knaves?

Alas! I'm but a nameless wight,
Trode i' the mire out o' sight!
But could I like Montgomeries fight,
　　Or gab like Boswell,
There's some sark-necks I wad draw tight,
　　An' tie some hose well.

God bless your Honours, can ye see't,
The kind, auld, cantie carlin greet,
An' no get warmly to your feet
　　An' gar them hear it?
An' tell them wi' a patriot-heat,
　　Ye winna bear it?

Some o' you nicely ken the laws
To round the period an' pause,
An' with rhetoric clause on clause
　　To mak harangues;
Then echo through Saint Stephen's wa's
　　Auld Scotland's wrangs.

Dempster, a true blue Scot I'se warran';
Thee, aith-detesting, chaste Kilkerran;
An' that glib-gabbed Highland Baron,
　　The Laird o' Graham;
An' ane, a chap that's damn'd auldfarran,
　　Dundas his name;

Erskine, a spunkie Norland billie;
True Campbells, Frederik an' Ilay;
An' Livingston, the bauld Sir Willie;
　　An mony ithers,
Whom auld Demosthenes or Tully
　　Might own for brithers.

Arouse, my boys! Exert your mettle
To get auld Scotland back her kettle;
Or faith! I'll wad my new plough-pettle,
　　Ye'll see't or lang,
She'll teach you, wi' a reekin whittle,
　　Anither sang.

This while she's been in crankous mood;
Her lost Militia fir'd her bluid
(Deil nor they never mair do guid
　　Play'd her that pliskie!)
An' now she's like to rin red-wud
　　About her whisky.

An' Lord, if ance they pit her till't,
Her tartan petticoat she'll kilt,
An' durk an' pistol at her belt,
　　She'll tak the streets,
An' rin her whittle to the hilt
　　I' th' first she meets!

For God sake, sirs! Then speak her fair,
An' straik her cannie wi' the hair,
An' to the muckle house repair,
　　Wi' instant speed
An' strive, wi' a' your wit an' lear,
　　To get remead.

Yon ill-tongu'd tinkler, Charlie Fox,
May taunt you wi' his jeers an' mocks;
But gie him't het, my hearty cocks!
    E'en cow the cadie,
An' send him to his dicing-box
    An sportin' lady.

Tell yon guid bluid o' auld Boconnock's
I'll be his debt twa mashlum bannocks,
An' drink his health in auld Nanse
  Tinnock's
    Nine times a week,
If he some scheme, like tea an' winnocks,
    Wad kindly seek.

Could he some commutation broach,
I'll pledge my aith in guid braid Scotch,
He need na fear their foul reproach
    Nor erudition,
Yon mixtie-maxtie queer hotch-potch,
    The Coalition.

Auld Scotland has a raucle tongue;
She's just a devil wi' a rung;
An' if she promise auld or young
    To tak their part,
Tho' by the neck she should be strung,
    She'll no desert.

An' now, ye chosen Five-and-Forty,
May still your Mither's heart support ye;
Then, though a minister grow dorty,
    An' kick your place,
Ye'll snap your fingers, poor an' hearty,
    Before his face.

God bless your Honours a' your days
Wi' soups o' kail an' brats o' claes,
In spite o' a' the thievish kaes
    That haunt St Jamie's!
Your humble poet sings an' prays,
    While Rab his name is.

POSTSCRIPT.

Let half-starv'd slaves in warmer skies
See future wines, rich-clust'ring, rise;
Their lot auld Scotland ne'er envies,
    But blythe an' frisky,
She eyes her free-born martial boys
    Tak aff their whisky.

What tho' their Phoebus kinder warms,
While fragrance blooms an' beauty charms,
When wretches range in famish'd swarms
    The scented groves,
Or, hounded forth, dishonour arms
    In hungry droves.

Their gun's a burden on their shouther;
They downa bide the stink o' powther;
Their bauldest thought's a hank'ring swither
    To stan' or rin,
Till skelp! A shot - they're aff, a' throu'ther,
    To save their skin.

But bring a Scotsman frae his hill,
Clap in his cheek a Highland gill,
Say 'Such is royal George's will,
    An' there's the foe!'
He has nae thought but how to kill
    Twa at a blow.

Nae cauld faint-hearted doubtings tease
    him;
Death comes, wi' fearless eye he sees him;
Wi' bluidy hand a welcome gies him;
    An' when he fa's,
His latest draught o' breathin' lea'es him
    In faint huzzas.

Sages their solemn een may steek,
An' raise a philosophic reek,
An' physically causes seek
    In clime an' season;
But tell me whisky's name in Greek,
    I'll tell the reason.

Scotland, my auld, respected mither!
Tho' whiles ye moistify your leather,
Till whaur ye sit on craps o' heather,
    Ye tine your dam;
Freedom and whisky gang thegither! —
    Tak' aff your dram!

This was written as a reaction to the Wash Act of 1784, which was designed to end duty free privileges of certain distillers, specifically Duncan Forbes of Culloden, who had been given exemption for political reasons in 1693. Forbes' Ferintosh whisky had become a by-word for Scotch whisky which was free from English taxation – a popular notion!

There is a theory that adverse taxation decisions like this one drove the Scottish distillers to devise more efficient production methods, which in the long run, worked to the benefit of the development of the industry.

The poem is an excellent example of Burns as political lobbyist. The language is witty and sharp and the subject obviously one he cares passionately about. Note the two-faced reference to 'damn'd Excisemen in a bussle'.

Tak Aff Your Dram

SYDNEY GOODSIR SMITH (1915-1975)

'Freedom and whisky gang thegither'
Or sae the Bardie sang-
Whisky sweet or whisky neat
Or whisky short or lang.

Ay, 'Freedom is a noble thing'
And whisky noble bree,
In Paradise they rin thegither
-Rivers o' whisky free!

For 'Whisky is the life o' man'
And whisky's what he lacks-
Wi' Scotland free the first we'd dae
Reduce the bluidy tax.

The wicked English ken this weel
And sae they haud us doon-
Ah, Scotland, ye could lead the world
Wi' the bottle at hauf-a-croun.

Then fetch tae me a pint o' malt!
Glenlivet be my stay!
Glenfiddich come, revive our soul
That dwynes wi' drouth away!

There's Mist in Islay, Mist in Skye,
And Cream in Inverness,
There's a Highland Park in the Northern
    Isles,
As Orkney men ken best.

I feel free....

Sing Gloag and Dewar, ring the Bells
O' bonnie St Johnstone on the Tay,
Ah, Crabbie, Crawford, Grant and Haig,
All noble names, support my lay.

Ah, Muse, whatever name ye bear
That dwells upon the Spey,
Gie us the wine o' libertie
Whas name is usquebae.

Then whisky gless or whisky pint
Or whisky dram or gill,
Breed aince again a hero race
Wi ilka man his still.

Ay, freedon and whisky be the cry
We'll sing wi three times three!
Come Scots wha hae and Scots wha hinna
And let us drink or dee!

The first part of this poem is built around some famous quotations. The title and first line come from the preceding poem by Robert Burns. From the 18th century to the present day, there is a recurring evocation of a lost time when people could distil whisky freely on a domestic scale – 'ilka man his still'. That may be a romantic notion but there is undoubtedly some justification for the widespread resentment of London-based taxation clumsily applied to an important Scottish industry.

Another example of how the Scots make comical complaints about taxation, supporting my theory that the burden of taxation is actually quite a useful hair shirt.

Twelve an' a Tanner a Bottle

WILL FYFFE

It's really high time, something was done
Tae alter the way that the country is run;
They're no daein' things in the way that
    they should,
Just take for instance the price o' the food –

For it's twelve an' a tanner a bottle
That's what it's costing today
Twelve an' a tanner a bottle
Man, it taks a' the pleasure away.
Before ye can hae a wee drappie,
You have tae spend a' that ye've got,
How can a fella be happy,
When happiness costs such a lot?

There's taxes on this, and taxes on that,
While the people grow thin, the officials
    grow fat,
And you have tae admit it's a bit under-
    hand,
Puttin' a tax on the breath o' the land

For it's twelve, &c.

Well I used tae meet wi' some auld pals o'
    mine,
When whisky was cheap, and it went doon
    like wine.
Noo I don't see them, I'm sorry tae tell,
Ah slip roond the corner and I drink by
    masel'

For it's twelve, &c.

This song refers to a time, during the Second World War, when increased taxation made the cost of whisky shoot up from about four shillings a bottle to twelve and sixpence. Until then, Scotsmen tended to drink a small whisky and a small beer – known as a 'nip and a chaser' or a 'hauf and a hauf'. When whisky became too expensive they started drinking pints of beer, like their English counterparts, saving one whisky for the end of the night. Thus did taxation policy change drinking patterns from that generation on.

Will Fyffe was a Music Hall performer who also had a song called 'The First Wee Drappie o' the Mornin'.

The Politician

ANGUS McINTYRE (1911-1986)

'Och times are hard in Barra',
You'd hear the Bodachs cry,
'No food to feed a sparra,
An' effery bottle dry'.

Old men, once fresh an' frisky,
So full of ploy and play,
Dropped dead for want of whisky,
– The plessed Uisque-bae.

Now, the dusty dry Sahara
Iss a bare an' barren land,
But the drought that year in Barra
Wass more than man could stand.

Aye, life was hard an' cruel,
And days were long an' sad,
When the strongest drink wass gruel
An' the war wass goin' bad.

A cleffer man, old Hector
An' wise the words he said,
'Wisout the barley's nectar
A man iss better dead.'

But strange the ways of Heaven,
When men in darkness grope;
Each sorrow has its leaven,
Each tragedy its hope.

The great ship, Politician,
Her hold stocked high wis grog,
Steamed proudly past the Island,
An' foundered in the fog.

A case was rent assunder,
Twelve bottles came to grief,
When the Barra surf, like thunder,
Came pounding on the Reef.

And then the scent of nectar
Came on the wild wind's breath,
'I smell it', screamed old Hector,
'It's whisky – sure as death'.

He yelled out, 'Kirsty, Kirsty,
bring down my oilskin coat;
No more will we be thirsty,
Salvation's in that boat'.

Tho' thirst her tongue had blistered,
Old Kirsty forced a laugh;
'I'm comin' too' she whispered,
'It's me that needs a half'.

Now Chon MacNeill wass dying;
The death that's far the worst;
No end so sad an' tryin'
As the fatal pangs of thirst.

For weeks he had been lying,
Wisout a sign of life,
An' all the neighbours crying
For his nearly widowed wife.

He sobbed, 'I am delivered,
From torture I am free',
As his nostrils flared an' quivered
In the glory from the Sea.

He shook chust like an aspen
The man they thought was dead,
An' sighin', gulpin', gaspin',
He vaulted out of bed.

Barefooted, in his nightie,
He slipped from out of their reach,
Wis steps bose long an' mighty
He headed for the beach.

Now, Sarah Chane MacKinnon,
- A lady through an' through,
Wass chust a wee bit partial
To a drop of Mountain Dew.

She brooded at the ingle,
Her form all old an' bent,
When her blood began to tingle
At a well-remembered scent.

Wan sniff an' she wass rising,
Two sniffs an' straight outside,
Where odours appetising
Were blowing from the tide.

By chove, she went full throttle
Across the Barra turf,
When she heard a tinkling bottle,
In the thunder of the surf.

She ran, but so did others,
Och hundreds, maybe more,
As Uncles, cousins, brothers,
Stampeded for the shore.

The boats were gaily dashing
Across the crested wave;
The long oars dipping, splashing
To their Alladin's cave.

They climbed aboard the liner,
The halt, the lame, the old,
No Vikings e'er were finer
No Pirates half so bold.

They peered wiz anzious faces,
Within the gaping hold,
An' saw a thousand cases,
Of precious, liquid gold.

'A shame, A shame,' cried Kirsty,
'It iss an act of God,
Chust think of Barra, thirsty,
An' all this goin' abroad'.

Och, the Ceilidhs, och, the pleasure,
Och the choy in Castlebay,
As the gurglin', golden treasure
Chased the cares of war away.

Och, the bottles that were hidden,
Buried deep beneath the croft;
Oh, the cases in the midden
Och, the choy up in the loft.

Who would heed an air-raid warning,
Who would hide himself in fright?
Wis a tumbler in the morning
An' a bumper late at night.

An' Barra boys, hard fighting
On sea and ocean wide,
Deserved their wee bit parcel
Wis glook, glook, glook inside.

Old Hector cried, 'We're winning,
The fact is plain to me,
This night is the beginning
Of victory at sea.'

He swigged another Chug-full,
An' happily he sighed,
'The Germans sure have had it,
Now Barra's fortified'.

'A Slainte now for Churchill,
His name I proudly call,
But the Barra Politician
Is the greatest of them all.'

The true story of the wreck of the S. S. Politician in the Sound of Eriskay in the morning of 5 February 1941 is actually every bit as interesting as any of the fiction that it inspired. That story is told by Roger Hutchinson in his fascinating book 'Polly'. Islanders found 22,000 cases of whisky in the hold of the stricken ship and a legend was born.

Compton Mackenzie reworked the story into 'Whisky Galore' and a film followed. Angus McIntyre was simply carrying on a tradition. More recently there has been a play

on the subject and Ian Davison has a song on the subject called 'Whisky on the Rocks'.

Whereas Compton Mackenzie changed the name of the ship to S. S. Cabinet Minister and the island to that of Little Todday, McIntyre has reverted to Politician but the island becomes Barra, (I have absolutely no doubt that the folk from Barra were involved, but the wreck was between Eriskay and South Uist).

In any event, not since the days of Ferintosh, has anything stimulated the Scots' imagination or tickled their sense of

humour and justice as much as the thought of plundering an ocean of free whisky from the hold of an English ship heading for America.

Angus McIntyre was a larger-than-life character from Argyll. He also wrote a poem about the fact that Islay Cheese was banned in Italy because of its supposed aphrodisiac qualities. Now there are more than half a dozen Islay products which could easily have the effect of increasing the birth rate in Italy, but believe me, Islay Cheese is not one of them.

The De'il's Awa' wi' th' Exciseman

ROBERT BURNS (1759-1796)

The Deil cam' fiddlin' through the toon,
And he's danced awa' wi' th' Exciseman,
And ilka wifie cries: – 'Auld Mahoun,
Ach, I wish you luck o' the prize man!'

The Deil's awa', the Deil's awa',
The Deil's awa' wi' th' Exciseman!
He's danced awa', he's danced awa',
He's danced awa' wi' th' Exciseman!

We'll mak' our maut, and we'll brew our drink,
And we'll dance, and sing, and rejoice, man,
And mony braw thanks to the muckle black Deil,
That's danced awa' wi' th' Exciseman.

The Deil's awa', &c.

There's threesome reels, and there's foursome reels,
And there's hornpipes and strathspeys, man,
But the best dance ever tae cam' tae the land
Was – the Deil's awa' wi' th' Exciseman.

The Deil's awa', &c.

The exciseman was responsible for insuring tax was paid on whisky. Naturally he was a universally hated figure in Scotland.

Burns was one himself, yet here he is writing about the exciseman being carried off by the devil, much to the delight of the local folk. (Burns was always big enough to contain contradictions!).

Apparently, he wrote this song while waiting for reinforcements to arrive so that he and his excise colleagues could arrest some smugglers off the Solway coast. He sang it at the excise dinner the following month, but there is no record of how appreciative his colleagues were. They were probably all drunk on confiscated whisky!

The Exciseman in a Coal Pit

TRADITIONAL

I know that young folk like to hear a new
    song
Of something that's funny and not very
    long
Concerning an exciseman, the truth I will
    tell
Who thought one night he was landed in
    hell.
An sing Fal de dal day dal dadie i-doo.

The exciseman went out for to look for his
    prey
He met two or three smugglers upon the
    highway
And gauging their liquors they had got to
    sell
The exciseman got drunk for the truth I
    will tell.
An sing Fal de dal day dal dadie i-doo.

He got so drunk that he fell to the ground
And like a fat sow he was forced to lie down
Just nigh to a coal pit the exciseman did lie
When four or five colliers by chance passed
    by.
An sing Fal de dal day dal dadie i-doo.

They shouldered him up and they carried
    him away
Like a pedlar's pack, without any delay
And into a bucket they handed him down
This jolly exciseman they got underground.
An sing Fal de dal day dal dadie i-doo.

The exciseman awoke in a terrible fear
Up started a collier, says 'What brought you
    here?'
'Indeed Mr Devil I don't very well know
But I think I am come to regions below.'
An sing Fal de dal day dal dadie i-doo.

'O what was you then in the world above?'
'O I was a gauger and few did me love
But indeed Mr Devil the truth I will tell
For since I've got here I shall be what you
    will.'
An sing Fal de dal day dal dadie i-doo.

'O then' said the collier 'it's here ye'll
  remain
Ye'll never get out of this dark cell again
For the gates they are shut and they'll bind
  you secure
All this you must suffer for robbing the
  poor.'
An sing Fal de dal day dal dadie i-doo.

'O Mr Devil have pity on me
I'll ne'er go a-robbing the poor you shall
  see
If you would look over as you've done
  before
I'll ne'er go a-robbing the poor any more.'
An sing Fal de dal day dal dadie i-doo.

'Then give us a guinea to drink with
  demand
Before you get back to a Christian land'
'O yes Mr Devil' the gauger did say
'For I long to get back to see the light of
  day.'
An sing Fal de dal day dal dadie i-doo.

In this song, the exciseman is not only drinking the whisky that he is supposed to capture, but he is stupid enough to be taken in by a rather transparent ruse. So we see yet again, that the exciseman is both wicked and simple. Who could have any sympathy for such an execrable rogue?

The Battle of Corrymuckloch

TRADITIONAL

December on the twenty-first a party o' our Scottish Greys
Gaed up among our mountaineers some whisky from them for to seize
Wi' sword and pistol by their side they thocht to mak a bold attack
And a' they wanted was to seize poor Donald wi' his smuggl'd drap.

Dirim a doo, a doo, a do, dirim a doo a daddie O
An' a' they wanted there to find was Donald and his smuggl'd drap.

The gauger and the Greys cam' on and they poor Donald did surroun'
He says 'Your whisky I maun seize by virtue of the British Crown'.
'Hoot, toot!' quo Donald 'no sae fast ye ken the whisky is her nain
She fearna you, nor your grey horse nor yet your muckle bearded men'.

Dirim a doo, a doo, a do, &c.

Then Donald and his men drew up an' Donald he did gi'e command;
An' a' the arms poor Donald had was just a stick in ilka hand.
An' when poor Donald's men drew up a guid stane dyke was at their back
Sae when their sticks tae prounach went wi' stanes they made a bold attack.

Dirim a doo, a doo, a do, &c.

An' ere the action it was o'er there fell a horseman on the plain
Quo Sandy unto Donald syne, - 'Ye've killed ane o' the bearded men'.
But up he gat an' left his horse and straight to Amulree he flew
And left the rest to do their best as they were left at Waterloo.

Dirim a doo, a doo, a do, &c.

But Donald and his men stuck fast an' garr'd the beardies quit the field
The gauger he was thumped weel afore his pride would let him yield
Then Donald's men they a' cried out 'Ye nasty filthy gauger loon,
If ye come back, ye'll ne'er win hame, to see your Ouchterarder Toon'.

Dirim a doo, a doo, a do, &c.

And when the battle it was o'er and not a horseman to be seen
Quo' Donald syne unto his men 'Ye'll sit ye a' doun on the green,
For noo my lads we'll hae a took shust o' the gear sic likes we hae;
Aye that's right', quo Donald 'but I'm sure they got a filthy hurry doon the
    brae'.

Dirim a doo, a doo, a do, &c.

There are many tales from the whisky wars - confrontations between the whisky makers and smugglers and the evil forces of the Crown. Stuart McHardy has gathered many of these tales in his book 'Tales of Whisky and Smuggling'. The common folk were always on the side of the whisky makers. These tales are probably the nearest thing Scotland has to the Robin Hood stories south of the border.

This song tells the story of a confrontation which actually took place in Perthshire early in the 19th century.

Atholl Brose

ROBERT LOUIS STEVENSON (1850-1894)

Willie and I cam doun by Blair
And in by Tullibardine;
The Rye were at the riverside,
An' bee-skeps in the garden;
I saw the reek o' a private still –
Says I 'Gude Lord, I thank ye!'
As Willie and I cam in by Blair,
And out by Killiecrankie.

Ye hinny bees, ye smuggler lads,
Thou Muse, the bard's protector,
I never kent what rye was for
Till I had drunk the nectar!
And shall I never drink it mair?
Gude troth, I beg your pardon!
The neist time I come doun by Blair
And in by Tullibardine.

F. Marian McNeill, in her book 'The Scots Cellar', gives a number of recipes for Atholl Brose, some have cream and some have oatmeal, but the fundamental two ingredients are whisky and honey.

She also gives two legends about the origin of Atholl Brose. One involves the heiress of Tullibardine, who was being intimidated by a wild fellow on her walks along the banks of the Tay. The wild man had killed a number of people and was proving very difficult to catch. One gallant young man sought his fortune by trapping the wild man, which he did by emptying the stone cup which provided his daily drink and filling it instead with whisky and honey. Naturally the monster of the woods got inebriated and was captured like a kitten. The young man married the heiress and they all lived happily ever after. George and the Dragon and Cyclops all rolled into one!

Stevenson seems to have been aware of the legend but his reference to the private still suggests a much more realistic clue to the origin of Atholl Brose, for whisky from an illicit still might well be almost undrinkable without the addition of some honey.

A concoction carefully made with good whisky, honey, a little oatmeal and a little cream sounds more like Ambrosia rather than Brose.

Tom McEwan, in his poem 'Athol Brose' says, 'Athol Brose, at evenings close, will mak' dune men like new'.

Shining Clear

ROBERT LOUIS STEVENSON / ALAN REID

A mile an' a bittock, a mile or twa,
Abune the burn, ayont the law,
Davie an' Donal' an' Charlie an' a',
An' the mune was shinin' clearly!

Ane went hame wi' the ither, an' then
The ither went hame wi' the ither twa men,
An' baith wad return him the service again,
An' the mune was shinin' clearly!

It's oot o' the barn and ower the hill,
Through the dark and there's the still
A cup in your hand and drink your fill
And the moon was shinin' clear.

The clocks were chappin' in house an' ha',
Eleeven, twal, an' ane an' twa;
An' the guidman's face was turnt to the wa',
An' the mune was shinin' clearly!

A wind got up frae affa the sea,
It blew the stars as clear's could be,
It blew in the een of o' a' the three,
An' the mune was shinin' clearly!

It's oot o' the barn...

Noo, Davie was first to get sleep in his head,
'The best o' frien's maun twine,' he said;
'I'm weariet, an' here I'm awa' to my bed.'
An' the mune was shinin' clearly!

Twa o' them walkin' and crackin' their lane,
The mornin' licht cam grey an' plain,
An' the birds they yammert on stick an'
        stane,
An' the mune was shinin' clearly!

It's oot o' the barn...

O years ayont, O years awa',
My lads, ye'll mind whate'er befa' -
My lads, ye'll mind on the bield o' the law,
When the mune was shinin' clearly.

It's oot o' the barn...

This is the enigmatic poem 'A Mile and a Bittock', by Stevenson, to which Alan Reid has added a tune and a chorus. Whatever Stevenson was writing about it's got something to do with male bonding through nocturnal adventure. Alan's chorus makes it clear that the poem is about a visit to an illicit still, which chimes in nicely with the previous poem.

Donal' Don

TRADITIONAL

Wha hasna heard o' Donal' Don,
Wi' a' his tanterwallops on;
I trow, he was a lazy drone,
    And smuggled Hieland whisky, O.

When first he cam' to auld Dundee,
'Twas in a smeeky hole lived he;
Where gauger bodies cou'dna see,
    He played the king a pliskie, O.

When he was young an' in his prime,
He lo'ed a bonnie lassie fine;
She jilted him, and aye sin' syne
    He's dismal, dull, and dusky, O.

A bunch o' rags is a' his braws,
His heathery wig wad fricht the craws;
His dusky face and clorty paws
    Wad fyle the Bay o' Biscay, O.

He has a sark, he has but ane,
It's fairly worn to skin an' bane,
A' loupin', like to rin its lane,
    Wi' troopers bauld and frisky, O.

Whene'er his sark's laid oot to dry,
The blockhead in his bed maun lie,
An' wait till a' the troopers die,
    Ere he gangs oot wi' whisky, O.

Yet, here's a health to Donal' Don,
Wi' a' his tanterwallops on;
An' may he never want a scone
    While he mak's Hieland whisky, O.

Even a character as wild and uncouth as Donal' Don, is held in general affection if he happens to make a bit of peat-reek in his 'smeeky hole'.

The Ewi wi' the Crookit Horn

TRADITIONAL

Were I but able to rehearse
My ewie's praise in proper verse,
I'd sound it out as loud and fierce
As ever piper's drone could blaw.

The ewie wi' the crookit horn,
A' that kent her micht hae sworn
Ne'er was sic a ewie born,
Here aboots or far awa'.

I neither needed tar nor keel
To mark her upon hip or heel;
Her crookit horn it did as weel
Tae ken her by amang them a'.

She never threatened scab nor rot,
But keepit aye her ain jog trot,
Baith to the fauld and to the cot,
Was never sweir to lead nor ca'.

The ewie wi', &c.

When ither ewies lap the dyke
And ate the kail for a' the tyke,
My ewie never played the like
But stayed ahint the barn wa'.

I lookit aye at even for her.
Lest mishanter should come owre her
Or the fumart should devour her
Gin the beastie bade awa'.

The ewie wi', &c.

Yet Monday last for a' my keeping
I canna speak it without greetin' –
A villain cam' when I was sleepin'
And stole my ewie, horn an' a'.

I socht her sair upon the morn,
And doun beneath a buss of thorn
I got my ewie's crookit horn,
But my ewie was awa'!

The ewie wi', &c.

But gin I had the loon that did it,
I hae sworn as weel as said it,
Though a' the world should forbid it,
I wad gie his neck a thraw.

For a' the claith that we had worn
Frae her and hers sae aften shorn,
The loss o' her we could ha'e borne,
Had fair strae-death ta'en her awa'.

The ewie wi', &c.

But silly thing tae lose her life
Aneath a greedy villain's knife;
I'm really feared that oor goodwife
Sall never win aboon't ava'.

Oh all ye bards benorth Kinghorn,
Call up your muses, let them mourn;
Our ewie wi' the crookit horn,
Is frae us stown and felled an' a'.

The ewie wi', &c.

The ewie wi' the crookit horn is traditionally used to symbolise the domestic (and hence illegal) whisky still. Certainly a ewie that always 'stayed ahint the barn wa'' would be a very unusual animal in reality. The words are sometimes attributed to the Rev. John Skinner and it may be that the hand of a minister explains the considerable ambiguity in the song.

Tak' it Man Tak' it

DAVID WEBSTER (1787-1837)

When I was a miller in Fife,
Losh! I thought that the sound o' the
    happer
Said, 'Tak' hame a wee flow to your wife,
To help to mak' brose to your supper'.
Then my conscience was narrow and pure,
But someway by random it rackit;
For I lifted twa neivefu' or mair,
While the happer said, 'Tak' it, man,
    tak' it'

Then hey for the mill and the kiln,
The garland and gear for my cogie;
And hey for the whisky and yill,
That washes the dust frae my craigie.

Although it's been lang in repute
For rogues to mak' rich by deceiving,
Yet I see that it disna weel suit
Honest men to begin to the theiving.
For my heart it gaed dunt upon dunt,
Oh, I thought ilka dunt it wad crack it;
Sae I flang frae my neive what was in't,
Still the happer said, 'Tak' it, man, tak' it'

Then hey for the mill, &c.

A man that's been bred to the plough,
Might be deav'd wi' its clamorous clapper;
Yet there's few that would suffer the sough,
After kennin' what's said by the happer.
I whiles thought it scoffed me to scorn,
Saying, 'Shame is your conscience no
    chackit?'
But when I grew dry for a horn,
It chang'd aye to 'Tak'it, man, tak' it'.

Then hey for the mill, &c.

The smugglers whiles cam' wi' their pocks,
'Cause they kent that I likit a bicker,
Sae I bartered whiles wi' the gowks,
Gied them grain for a sowp o' their liquor.
I had lang been accustomed to drink,
And aye when I purposed tae quat it,
That thing wi' its clappertie clink
Said aye to me 'Tak' it, man, tak' it'.

Then hey for the mill, &c.

But the warst thing I did in my life,
Nae doot but you'll think I was wrang o't;
Od! I tauld a bit bodie in Fife
A' my tale, and he made a bit sang o't.
I have aye had a voice a' my days,
But for singin' I ne'er gat the knack o't;
Yet I try whyles, just thinking to please
The greedy, wi' 'Tak' it, man, tak' it'.

Then hey for the mill, &c.

Now, miller and a' as I am,
This far I can see through the matter:
There's men mair notorious to fame,
Mair greedy than me or the muter.
For 'twad seem that the hale race o' men,
Or wi' safety, the hauf we maun mak' it,
Ha'e some speakin' happer within,
That said to them, 'Tak' it, man, tak' it'.

Then hey for the mill, &c.

There is no doubt that dry, dusty work makes a body thirsty. The sound of the happer is both the inner 'bad voice' and the rhythm that drives the tune. There is a classic barter exchange here where the miller gives some grain to the whisky smugglers in return for whisky. The grain of course will then be turned into whisky at some secret location.

Glaisca Whisky

J. LIVINGSTON (1858-?)

Come all ye folks who weary are
O' life, its cares and trouble,
Who anything will do and dare
So you may burst the bubble;
I have a plan within my head
That's new and nothing risky,
Whene'er you want to nick the thread,
Just try oor Glaisca whisky.

Try oor Glaisca whisky;
Try oor Glaisca whisky;
It gies us pleasure wi' our death,
So hey for Glaisca whisky!

A plunge in Clyde's no just the thing;
But people who are dreary
May into it themselves gae fling,
But I'm for something cheery.
The knife - the name o't gars me grue,
An' mak's my face look dusky;
But I prefer the barley broo,
An' stick to Glaisca whisky.

Try oor Glaisca, &c.

Death by the rape - weel, I'm no sure
But I'd prefer't to mony;
But then, my frien's, a dance in air
Is onything but bonny;
So they may hang themselves wha will,
But I'm for something frisky -
Hey, landlord, fetch anither gill
O' hame-made Glaisca whisky.

Try oor Glaisca, &c.

The pooshin stuffs the doctors sell
You scarcely can get ony,
But Glaisca whisky bears the bell,
It's flavoured wi' sae mony;
An' pooshin sellin's sae fenced roun',
To buy it is but risky;
But ye may cut throats, hang, or droon,
When primed wi' Glaisca whisky!

Try oor Glaisca, &c.

I found this song in Nimmo's 'Songs and Ballads of Upper Clydesdale'. The tune is unknown. The note there says it was written after the author read an analysis of Glasgow whisky in the Mail. The true account of the Victorian scandal involving the sale of adulterated whisky in public houses and dram shops in Glasgow is told in Edward Burns book 'Bad Whisky'. The adulteration of whisky is one of the inevitable consequences of heavy taxation.

It may also have something to do with the greed of sellers and the poverty of customers.

I was served a carry-out of 'draft whisky' in a lemonade bottle by a publican in Blackpool just a few years ago, so this kind of thing still happens.

Ye'd Sook it Through a Clarty Cloot

MEN AND WOMEN: THE OTHER WHISKY BATTLEGROUND

For quite a long time in Scotland, women were pretty well excluded from drinking establishments. Being women, of course, they've always had to find slightly unorthodox ways of getting what they want, and in the procurement of liquor, being excluded from pubs never seems to have handicapped them too much. Indeed it may be that one of their roles, historically, has been in the making of drink. Many songs have reference to ale-wives and women who keep inns. There is not much evidence of their being involved in the distilling of whisky in the early days, but certainly the record has them involved in the selling and the smuggling of the stuff. 'Bung Your Eye' is a good example, and there are stories about characters like Jean Anderson who smuggled whisky in bladders hidden under her skirts.

There is certainly no shortage of songs and poems about women who drink. Some drink impressive amounts, some behave outrageously and some are a trial to their poor husbands – in other words anything men can do women can do just as well, or as badly.

There is, however, no denying that in the majority of songs and poems the women tend to play a non-drinking role. This is certainly true in most of the songs with a Temperance message. Most of the members of the Temperance organisations were women and children, and the women's roles tend to be fairly consistent – women are the justified naggers or victimised bullies. We find them putting up with terrible privations and unacceptable behaviour as a result of the drinking problems of their men. They only stay in the relationship for the children or out of a sense of decency and marital rectitude. Usually something happens to spur them into action and when roused they are strong, articulate, wise and fearsome individuals who can have their men shaking in their shoes. Very often as a result of their words and actions, the men see the light and give up the drink.

Bung Your Eye

TRADITIONAL

A jolly exciseman was walking the street
When a brisk young damsel he chanced for
   to meet
As she drew nigh she said will you buy?
Pray what do you sell? And she said Bung
   your eye.
Dirry down down hey dirry down.

Bung your eye says the exciseman what
   mean you by that?
Good Highland Whisky I'm sure ye may
   guess
We live in a cottage where it's made by
And we give a name which is Bung your eye.
Dirry down down hey dirry down.

If ye be a gentleman as ye do appear
To leave you my basket I'll never fear
Till I speak to a friend that is standing
   near by
And I'll leave you in charge sir o' my Bung
   your eye.
Dirry down down hey dirry down.

But hearken a moment what I am to
   mention
To look in the basket it was my intention
In a moment or two a young child did cry
And up in my arms I took young Bung
   your eye.
Dirry down down hey dirry down.

Up with the child and home I went
For to get it christened it was my intent
O yes says the parson we'll christen't by and
   by
Pray what is the name and I said Bung
   your eye.
Dirry down down hey dirry down.

Bung your eye said the parson that is an
   odd name
O yes sir but an odd way it came
And all ye young men as ye do pass by
Ye may call me the father o' young Bung
   your eye.
Dirry down down hey dirry down.

So all ye excisemen that walk on the street
Beware o' young damsels that you chance to
    meet
With their good Highland Whisky they look
    very shy
And they'll make you the father to their
    Bung your Eye.
Dirry down down hey dirry down.

The first version of this song I ever heard was called 'Quare Bugle Rye', sung by The Dubliners. In that song the lad who was taken advantage of by the cheeky lass was a sailor called Jack. The various Scottish versions, naturally cast the exciseman as the only kind of man stupid and greedy enough to be duped in this way.

149

Brebster Ceilidh

DAVID MORRISON

Tam went to the ceilidh
    wanting a lass to lie under him.
Councillor Jones went to the ceilidh
        to show that he had concern
        for the local community,
        (and to catch votes for the coming local
            election).
Young Bess, thirsting for romance
        went to the ceilidh
        thinking she might win her knight,
        all white and rosy-cheeked.
Auld Martha went to the ceilidh
        to reassure herself about the sin
        and wayward ways of young ones.
And Sam; why did he go?
        to get drunk on other people's whisky.

All through the evening the dance raged
And the booze flowed as a demon
        catching many a soul for Hell.

In the morning, Tam was wet
        with the lack of a woman.
Councillor Jones awoke with a thick head
        remembering only too well
        that he had annoyed
        those he should not have annoyed.
Young Bess, poor lass, looked in the
            mirror
        and saw the bruises on her neck;
        she feared the time of month.
Auld Martha resolved to see the Reverend Gunn
        about the sin in his parish.

And Sam, what happened to Sam?
    In the morning, Sam, still drinking,
    Thought kindly of the young lass
    who had lain for him;
    He thought of the many
    who had called him fine fellow;
    He laughed as he thought of Auld
        Martha saying –
        That's guid o' ye, Sam,
        Tae see young Bess hame.
        Ye're a fine man, Sam –
        She'll no come tae ony hairm
        In your care.

Sam, drinking other people's whisky
    the morning after the night afore
    knew a Heaven as he crawled on the
        floor.

There is a dark edge to this poem, which nonetheless catches a reality often found in Northern village ceilidhs.

Donal' Blue

TRADITIONAL

My name is Donal' Blue, an ye ken me fu' weel,
Straik me canny by the hair, I'm a quiet, simple chiel',
But gin ye rouse the bear, I'm as rouch as the deil,
Gin I get a claucht o' yer noddle.

But I'll tell ye o' a trick, man, that happened in the south,
A smith got a wife, an' she had an unco drouth;
She liket it sae weel, put sae muckle in her mouth,
She was aften helpet hame in the mornin'.

So it happen'd ae day, when the smith he was thrang,
They brocht a wife till him - a wife that couldna gang;
He took her on his back, an' up the stair he ran,
An' flang her on the bed wi' a fury.

He lockit the door, brocht the key in his han',
And cam' doon the stair cryin', 'Oh, bewitched man;
This conduct o' hers I'm no fit to stan' -
I'll list for a sodger in the mornin'.'

He fell to his wark - he was shoein' at a horse;
They cried 'Tak' in your wife, smith, she's lyin' at the Cross.'
He lifted up his hammer, and strack wi' siccan force,
He knocket doon the studdy in his fury.

'The deil's in the folk! What do they mean ava?
Gin I've ae drucken wife, Lo'd! I'm no needin' twa;'
But they cried aye the louder, 'Tak' her in frae the snaw,
Or surely she will perish ere the mornin'.'

So the smith he gaed oot, an' viewed her a' roun';
'By my sooth, and it's her; but hoo did she win doon?'
He hoisted her awa' on his back up to the room,
Whaur the ither wife was lyin' soondly snorin'.

The smith, to his surprise, coulda tell which was his,
Frae the tap to the tae they were dressed in a piece:
An' sae close they resembled each ither in the face,
He couldna tell which was his Jeannie.

'Deil-ma-care,' says the smith, 'let them baith lie still,
When ance she is sober, she'll surely ken hersel'.'
Noo, frae that day to this Jeannie never buys a gill,
Nor will she weet her mou' in the mornin'.

A rather unlikely tale this, but a comical one, and the kind of story which would have delighted many a ceilidh in the old days.

Drap of Capie – O

TRADITIONAL

There lived a wife in our gate-end,
She lo'ed a drap o' capie - O,
And all the gear that ere she gat,
She slipt it in her gabie - O.

Upon a frosty winter's night,
The wife had got a drapie - O;
And she had pish'd her coats sae weil,
She could not find the patie - O.

But she's awa' to her goodman,
They ca'd him Tamie Lamie - O.
Gae ben and fetch the cave to me,
That I may get a dramie - O.

Tamie was an honest man,
Himself he took a drappie - O,
It was nae weil out o'er his craig,
Till she was on his tapie - O.

She paid him weil, baith back and side,
And fair she creish'd his backie - O,
And made his skin baith blue and black,
And gar'd his shoulders crackie - O.

Then he's awa' to the malt barn,
And he has ta'en a pockie - O,
And put her in, baith head and tail,
And cast her o'er his backie - O.

The carling spurn'd wi' head and feet,
The carle he was sae ackie - O,
To ilka wall that he came by,
He gar'd her head play knackie - O.

Goodman, I think you'll murder me,
My brains you out will knockie - O,
He gi'd her aye the other hitch,
Lie still, you devil's buckie - O.

Goodman, I'm like to make my burn,
O let me out, good Tamie - O;
Then he set her upon a stane,
And bade her pish a damie - O.

Then Tamie took her aff the stane,
And put her in the pockie - O,
And when she did begin to spurn,
He lent her aye a knockie - O.

Away he went to the mill-dam,
And there ga'e her a duckie - O,
And ilka chiel that had a stick,
Played thump upon her backie - O.

And when he took her hame again,
He did hing up the pockie - O,
At her bed-side, as I hear say,
Upon a little knagie - O.

And ilka day that she up-rose,
In naething but her smockie - O,
Sae soon as she look'd o'er the bed,
She might behold the pockie - O.

Now all ye men, baith far and near,
That have a drunken tutie - O,
Duck your wives in time of year,
And I'll lend you the pockie - O.

The wife did live for nineteen years,
And was fu' frank and cuthie - O,
And ever since she got the duck,
She never had the druthie - O.

At last the carling chanc'd to die,
And Tamie did her bury - O,
And for the publick benefit,
He has gar'd print the curie - O.

And this he did her motto make;
Here lies an honest luckie - O,
Who never left the drinking trade,
Until she got a duckie - O.

There is a shorter version of this song in Greig–Duncan, (Volume 3), which has the addition of a chorus –
'My little lamb O doo O
My little lamb O daddie O.'
An excellent story, in spite of its wife-beating (which echoes other songs like 'The Wife in the Wether's Skin' or 'The Wee Cooper o' Fife'). Actually, in this case it was definitely the wife who started it. I think he went a bit too far in the end, but it did have the desired effect.

155

The Wee Wifukie

DR. ALEXANDER GEDDES (1737-1802)

There was a wee bit wifukie was comin' frae
  the fair,
Had got a wee bit drappukie, that bred her
  meikle care;
It gaed about the wifie's heart, and she
  began tae spew,
Oh! quo' the wee wifukie, I wish I binna
  fou.
  I wish I binna fou, quo she, I wish I binna fou.
  Oh! Quo' the wee wifukie, I wish I binna fou.

If Johnnie find me barley-sick, I'm sure
  he'll claw my skin;
But I'll lie down an' tak' a nap before that I
  gae in.
Sitting at the dykeside, and taking o' her
  nap,
By came a packman laddie wi' a little pack.
  Wi' a little pack, quo' she, wi' a little pack,
  By came a packman laddie wi' a little pack.

He's clippit a' her gowden locks sae bonnie
  and sae lang:
He's ta'en her purse and a' her placks, and
  fast awa' he ran;
And when the wifukie waken'd up her head
  was like a bee,
Oh! quo the wee wifukie, this is nae me.
  This is nae me, quo' she, this is nae me,
  Somebody has been felling me, and this is nae me.

When I was bonny Bessukie, my locks were
  like the gowd,
And I look'd like ony lassukie, sic times as
  they were cowed.
And Johnnie was aye tellin' me I was richt
  fair to see;
And somebody has been felling me, and
  this is nae me.
  This is nae me, quo' she, this is nae me,
  Somebody has been felling me, and this is nae me.

I met wi' kindly company, and birl'd my
  bawbee!
And still, if this be Bessukie, three placks
  remain wi' me,
But I will look the pursie nooks, see gin the
  cunyie be: –
There's neither purse nor plack about me!
  – this is nae me.
  This is nae me, quo' she, this is nae me,
  Somebody has been felling me, and this is nae me.

I have a little housukie, but, and a kindly
  man;
A dog, they ca' him Doussiekie; if this be
  me he'll fawn;
And Johnnie, he'll come to the door, and
  kindly welcome gi'e,
And a' the bairns on the floor will dance if
  this be me.
  But this is nae me, quo' she, this is nae me,
  Somebody has been felling me, and this is nae me.

The nicht was lang and dang oot weet, and
    oh but it was dark;
The doggie heard a body's foot, and he
    began to bark.
And when she heard the doggie bark, and
    kennin' it was he,
Oh, weel ken ye, Doussie, quo' she, this is
    nae me.
    This is nae me, quo' she, this is nae me,
    Somebody has been felling me, and this is nae me.

When Johnnie heard his Bessie's word, fast
    to the door he ran:
Is that you, Bessukie? – Wow, na, man!
Be kind to the bairns a', and weel may ye
    be;
And fareweel, Johnnie, quo' she, this is nae
    me!
    This is nae me, quo' she, this is nae me,
    Somebody has been felling me, and this is nae me.

John ran to the minister, his hair stood a'
    on end,
I've gotten sic a fricht, sir, I fear I'll never
    mend;
My wife's come hame without a head,
    crying out most piteously,
Oh, fareweel Johnnie, quo' she, this is nae
    me!
    This is nae me, quo' she, this is nae me,
    Somebody has been felling me, and this is nae me.

The tale you tell, the parson said, is
    wonderful to me,
How that a wife, without a head could
    speak, or hear, or see!
But things that happen hereabout so
    strangely alter'd be,
That I could maist wi' Bessie say, 'tis neither
    you nor she.
    Neither you nor she, quo' he, neither you nor she,
    Wow na, Johnnie man, 'tis neither you nor she.

Now Johnnie he cam' hame again, and oh!
    But he was fain
To see his little Bessukie come to hersel'
    again.
He got her sitting on a stool, wi' Tibbuk on
    her knee;
Oh! Come awa', Johnnie, quo' she, come
    awa' to me,
For I've got a nap wi' Tibbukie, and this is
    now me.
    This is now me, quo' she, this is now me,
    I've got a nap wi' Tibbukie, and this is now me.

Yet another wife with a drink problem. How do these poor men put up with it? I suppose the message in this song is that if you ha'e a wee drap whisukie, you're apt to lose the heidukie!

Tall Tale

WATT NICOL

I pu'd the cork fae the first bottle, had a little drink,
Kissed the bottle tenderly, poured it down the sink,
Uncorked the second, did the same as before,
Before I poured it down the sink, I drank a little more.
Uncorked the third and I drank a little toast
To the losing of the ten friends I really like the most.
Stood to attention, had another little drink,
Threw the cork in the bucket and the whisky down the sink.

Oh the next three bottles they were very quickly swilled,
As I uncorked the drainage, only drank a gill,
But the next one caught me for the cork was very tight,
The room was going round and round, which didn't help my plight.
I fought to gain my balances, I leaned against the wall,
I couldn't draw the room from the damn sink at all.
When at last I drew it, with a mighty plop,
Fell on my arse and I drank a glass of cork.

The eighth sink was different, for the glass was very slack.
I held the room with one hand and I knocked the bugger back.
I tried to count the empties as they danced before my eyes,
I'd only counted twenty three when much to my surprise,
There were ten sinks of whisky, every one uncorked,
The drain in the bottle it was very badly blocked.
Then I heard my wife, as on the door she knocked,
Fell in the bath tub, drank the bloody lot.

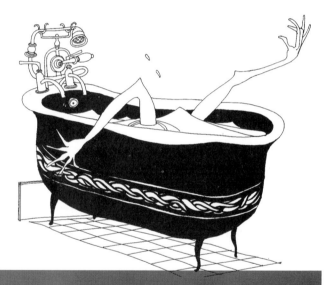

This song, in the style of some old ballads, starts in the fifth Act. The background to it is the wife discovering her husband's secret supply of whisky – ten green bottles – underneath the stair. As she does not approve of him drinking, she insists he has to pour them all down the sink, and the poor, bullied, hen– pecked soul has to do as she says. Naturally, he makes a small defiant gesture.

You can tell this is a Glasgow song by the humour, and by the fact that the woman is bigger and stronger than the man.

Tongue Discipline

DANIEL KING (1844-1891)

Yer fou, oh, Robin Duff, yer fou,
Ye haena got a fit tae stan',
The smell that's comin' frae yer mou'
Wad sicken ony sober man;
An' yet ye'll tell me tae ma cheek
'Twas harmless a' the drink ye got;
Preserve us, Rab, ye canna speak,
Ye leein', dirty, drunken sot.

I wonder what on earth ye mean,
Wi' sic a bonny cairry-on;
If ye'd a wife like Bogston Jean,
She'd smash yer nose as flat's a scone
Turn roon! Dear me! what claes wi' glaur!
Look at the picture o' yer coat!
Just lift yer han', man, if ye dare,
You cruel-hearted, drunken sot.

If ye was daein' what was richt,
Ye'd teach the bairns the fear o' God;
Ye canna, Rab, when ilka nicht
Yer stoatin' under sic a load.
Ye neither tend tae wife nor bairn,
For, haith, yer seldom aff the trot,
A feed o' drink's a' your concern,
Ye heedless, dirty, drunken sot.
Ye tell me aft tae shut ma mooth,

For fear the neebors hear me flite,
I've aften hid frae them the truth,
But noo I dinna care a dite.
Ye've ta'en it oot me gey'n sair,
Wi' tipplin' at the cursed tot,
An' noo ye'll bully me for mair,
Ye greedy, dirty, drunken sot.

Mony a weary nicht I've sat,
Aft wi' a gnawin', empty wame;
An' aften, aften hae I grat
To think ye made sic licht o' hame.
Yer weans are nearly starved to death,
But, Rab, ye dinna care a jot;
Oh, haud awa' frae me yer breath,
Ye heartless, dirty, drunken sot.

I've heard ye rin the whisky doon,
An' say it could be done withoot;
Ne'er say't again, ye drunken loon,
Ye'd sook it through a clarty cloot.
I wish I'd never seen your face,
If only I could loose the knot
That's brocht me tae sic black disgrace,
Ye laithsome, dirty, drunken sot.

Daniel King was born in Glasgow and was a shipyard worker.

Here is another strong woman giving her man a hard time!

Much of the temperance poetry is pretty poor, but this is a powerful piece of writing. It is possible that now and then the clear eye and brain of the tee-totaller almost compensates for their lack of whisky-derived inspiration, ecstasy and wit.

The Wag at the Wa'

TRADITIONAL

I've been hae'in a sociable nicht
Wi' my cronies a sociable crew,
Oh I've had a drink twa more or less,
And I begin tae suspect that I'm fou!
I'm no very sure where I am,
I'm raither the waur o' the drappie,
It's a quarter tae twa, the last bus is awa',
What does't matter as lang as I'm happy.

She's watchin the wag at the wa',
Cronies I'll hae tae be leavin',
My conscience, a quarter tae twa,
And I said I'd be hame at eleeven;
So cronies guid-nicht tae ye aa,
Losh, but I'm sweir tae gae 'wa,
But Mistress McCann's waitin up for her man
And she's watchin the wag at the wa'.

When I meet wi' they cronies o' mine,
And we've had a drammie or twa,
When the time comes tae pairt, man it gangs tae my hairt,
It's a thocht tae gang hame through the snaw;
When a pal puts his airm roond my neck,
And implores me tae bide a while langer,
If he prigs wi me sair, 'It's the wife', I declare,
'I wid stop but for fear o' her anger.'

She's watchin the wag at the wa', &c.

In some parts of Scotland a 'wag at the wa' is apparently a spirit of some kind, but in this song it is clearly a pendulum clock. The inner voice of the wife waiting at home is familiar to many drinking men. It brings to mind Kate O Shanter, 'nursing her wrath to keep it warm'. (If you want to hear how Kate's wrath expresses itself when Tam gets home – get hold of Matthew Fitt's poem 'Kate O Shanter's Tale').

Johnnie, my Man

TRADITIONAL

'O, Johnnie, my man, do you no think on risin'?
The day is far spent and the nicht's comin' on;
Your siller's near dune, and the stoup's toom afore ye;
O, rise up, my Johnnie, and come awa' hame'.

'O, wha is it that I hear speaking sae kindly?
I think it's the voice o' my ain wifie Jean;
Come in by, my dearie, and sit doon beside me,
It's time enough yet to be gaun awa' hame'.

'O, Johnnie, my man, when we first fell a-courting,
We had naething but love then to trouble our mind;
We spent a' our time 'mang the sweet scented roses,
And I ne'er thocht it lang then to gang awa' hame'.

'I remember richt weel, Jean, the time that ye speak o',
And weel I remember the sweet flowery glen;
But thae days are a' past, and will never return love,
Sae sit doon beside me, nor think o' gaun hame'.

'O, Johnnie, my man, the bairns are a' greetin',
Nae meal in the barrel to fill their wee wames;
While sittin' here drinkin', ye leave me lamentin';
O, rise up, my Johnnie, and come awa' hame'.

Then Johnnie he rase and he bang'd the door open,
Saying, 'Cursed be the tavern that e'er let me in;
And curs'd be the whisky that's made me sae frisky;
O, fare ye weel whisky, for I'm awa' hame'.

'And Jeannie, my dear, your advice will be taken,
I'll leave aff the auld deeds, and follow thee hame;
Live sober and wisely, and aye be respected;
Nae mair in the ale-house I'll sit, but at hame'.

Noo Johnnie goes oot ilka fine summer even,
Wi' his wife and his bairns, fu' trig and fu' bein,
Though a wee while sin' syne, in rags they were rinnin'
While Johnnie sat fu' in the ale house at e'en.

Contented and crouse, he sits by his ain fireside,
And Jeannie, a happier wife there is nane;
Nae mair to the tavern at nicht does he wander,
But's happy wi' Jean and his bairnies at hame.

A classic temperance story line, in which the errant husband is shamed by his wife into leaving the pub, facing up to his domestic responsibilities and giving up the drink for ever. I heard Ray Fisher introduce the song to an English audience by saying, 'this is what in Scotland we would call a fairy tale'.

Watty and Meg
or The Wife Reformed

ALEXANDER WILSON (1766-1823)

Keen the frosty winds were blawin'
Deep the sna' had wreath'd the ploughs,
Watty weary't a' day sawin',
Daunert down to Mungo Blew's.

Dyster Jock was sitting, cranky,
Wi' Pate Tamson o' the hill,
Come awa', quo Johnny, Watty,
Haith we'se ha' anither jill.

Watty, glad to see Jock Jabos,
And sae mony neibors roun',
Kicket frae his shoon the sna ba's,
Syne ayont the fire sat down.

Owre a board, wi' bonnocks heapet,
Cheese and stowps and glasses stood;
Some war roaring, ithers sleepet,
Ithers quietly chewt their cude.

Joke was selling Pate some tallow,
A' the rest a racket hel',
A' but Watty, wha, poor fellow,
Sat an' smoket by himsel'.

Mungo hil't him up a tooth-fu',
Drank his health and Mag's in ane,
Watty puffin' out a mouthfu',
Pledg't him wi' a dreary grane.

What's the matter, Watty, wi' you?
Trouth your chafts are fa'ing in
Something's wrang - I'm vext to see you -
Gude sake! But ye're desp'rate thin!

Aye, quo' Watty, things are alter't,
But it's past redemption now,
Lord, I wish I had been halter'd
When I marry'd Maggy How.

I've been poor, an' vext, and raggy,
Try't wi' troubles no that sma',
Them I bore - but marrying Maggy
Laid the cap'stane o' them a'.

Night and day she's ever yelpin,
Wi' the weans she ne'er can gree;
When she's tired wi' perfect skelpin',
Then she flees like fire on me.

See you, Mungo, when she'll clash on,
Wi' her everlasting clack,
Whyles I've had my neive, in passion,
Liftet up to break her back!

O, for gudesake, keep frae cuffets,
Mungo shook his head and said,
Weel I ken what sort o' life it's;
Ken ye, Watty, how I did?

After Bess and I was kippl't,
Fact she grew like ony bear,
Brak' my shins, and when I tippl't,
Harl't out my vera hair!

For a wee I quietly knuckl't,
But when naething wad prevail,
Up my claes and cash I buckl't,
Bess for ever fare ye weel.

Then her din grew less and less aye,
Fact I gart her change her tune;
Now a better wife than Bessy
Never stept in leather shoon.

Try this Watty – When ye see her
Raging like a roaring flood,
Swear that moment that ye'll lea'e her;
That's the way to keep her gude.

Laughing, sangs, and lasses' skirls,
Echo'd now out through the roof,
Done! quo Pate, and syne his airls
Nail't the dryster's wauket loof.

In the thrang o' stories-telling,
Shaking hauns, and ither cheer,
Swith! A chap comes on the hallen,
Mungo, is our Watty here?

Maggy's weel-kent tongue and hurry
Dartet thro' him like a knife,
Ope the door flew – like a fury
In came Watty's scawlin' wife.

Nasty, gude-for-naething being!
O ye snuffy, drucken sow!
Bringan wife and weans to ruin,
Drinkin' here wi' sic a crew!

Devil nor your legs were broken!
Sic a life nae flesh endures –
Toilan like a slave, to slocken
You, ye divor, and your whores!

Rise! ye drucken beast o' Bethel!
Drink's your night and day's desire:
Rise this precious hour, or faith I'll
Fling your whisky in the fire.

Watty heard her tongue unhalow'd,
Pay't his groat wi' little din,
Left the house while Maggy follow'd,
Flytin' a' the road behin'.

Fowk frae every door cam' lampin',
Maggie curs't them ane and a',
Clappit wi' her hauns, and stampin',
Lost her bachals i' the sna.

Hame at length, she turn'd the gavil,
Wi' a face as white's a clout,
Ragin' like the verra devil,
Kitchen stools and chairs about.

Ye'll sit wi' your limmers round you!
Hang you, Sir, I'll be your death!
Little hauds my hauns, confound you!
But I'll cleeve you to the teeth.

Watty, wha, 'midst this oration,
Ey'd her while but daurna speak,
Sat like patient resignation,
Trem'lan by the ingle cheek.

Sad his wee drap brose he sippet,
Maggy's tongue gaed like a bell,
Quietly to his bed he slippet,
Sighen aften to himsel'.

Nane are free frae some vexation,
Ilk ane has his ills to dree;
But through a' the hale creation,
Is a mortal vext like me!

A' night lang he rout and gauntet,
Sleep nor rest he cou'dna tak!
Maggy, aft wi' horror hauntet,
Mum'lin started at his back.

Soon as e'er the morning peepet,
Up raise Watty, waefu' chiel,
Kist his weanies while they sleepet,
Waukent Meg, and sought fareweel.

Farewell Meg! – and O! May heav'n
Keep you aye within his care,
Watty's heart ye've lang been grievin',
Now he'll never fash you mair.

Happy cou'd I been beside you,
Happy, baith at morn and e'en;
A' the ills did e'er betide you,
Watty aye turn't out your frien'.

But ye ever like to see me,
Vext and sighin', late and sair,
Farewell, Maggie, I've sworn to lea' thee,
So thou'll never see me mair.

Meg a' sabbin', sae to lose him,
Sic a change had never wist,
Held his haun close to her bosom
While her heart was like to burst.

O my Watty, will ye lea' me,
Frien'less, helpless, to despair!
O! For this ae time forgie me,
Never will I vex you mair.

Aye! Ye've aft said that, and broken
A' your vows ten times a week:
No, no, Meg! See there's a token,
Glittering on my bonnet cheek.

Ower the seas I march this morning,
Listet, testet, sworn an' a',
Forc'd by your confounded girning;
Fareweel, Meg! For I'm awa'.

Then poor Maggy's tears and clamour
Gusht afresh, and louder grew,
While the weans, wi' mournfu' yaummer,
Round their sabbin' mother flew.

Through the yirth I'll wander wi' you –
Stay, O Watty! Stay at hame,
Here upon my knees I'll gie you
Ony vow you like to name.

See your poor young lammies pleading?
Will you gang and break our heart!
No a house to put our head in!
No a friend to take our part?

Ilka word came like a bullet!
Watty's heart begoud to shake!
On a kist he laid his wallet,
Dightet baith his een and spake.

If aince mair I could, by writing,
Lea' the sodgers and stay still,
Wad you swear to drop your flyting?
Yes, O Watty, yes I will.

Then, quo Watty, mind, be honest;
Aye to keep your temper strive;
Gin you break this dredful promise,
Never mair expect to thrive.

Marget Howe! This hour ye solemn
Swear by every thing that's gude,
Ne'er again your spouse to scol' him,
While life warms your heart and blood.

That ye'll ne'er in Mungo's seek me,
Ne'er put drucken to my name,
Never out at e'ening seek me
Never gloom when I come hame.

That ye'll ne'er, like Bessy Miller,
Kick my shins, and rug my hair;
Lastly, I'm to keep the siller
This upo your soul you swear?

O-h! Quo' Meg, 'Aweel', quo Watty,
Fareweel! Faith, I'll try the seas,
O stan still, quo Meg, and grat aye
Ony ony way ye please.

Maggy syne, because he prest her,
Swore to a' thing owre again,
Watty lap, and danc't, and kist her;
Wow! But he was wondrous fain.

Down he threw his staff victorious;
Aff gaed bonnet, claes, and shoon;
Syne below the blankets, glorious,
Held anither Hinny-Moon.

I think the length of this makes it a poem rather than a song, though there is a tune in Greig–Duncan. Alexander Wilson was quite a character who had to flee to America to escape prosecution for his polemical poems and political affiliations. This piece was extremely popular, apparently selling 100,000 copies throughout Scotland.

You can draw you own moral lessons from this delightful tale. It does seem refreshing that it is the nagging wife who is transformed and not the poor husband dragged screaming to sobriety by the Temperance League.

Happy are we a' thegither

WHISKY AS LUBRICANT FOR SOCIAL OCCASIONS

From Burns Night to Hogmanay whisky is the drink of choice in Scotland for most toasts and cere-monial drinks. Champagne is increasingly found in this role, but there is room in Scotland for both. Indeed, since France now consumes more whisky than the UK, it is an important gesture, preserving the spirit of the Auld Alliance, that we should find a place on our table for the best of French fare. Also, champagne and whisky are perhaps the only two alcoholic drinks with enough dignity, quality and style to be suitable for consumption at any time, in any place and in any circumstances (including breakfast).

Between Hogmanay and Burns night, there is a slight chill in the air, while those who gave up drinking as a New Year resolution, still grit their teeth and cast a gloom around them. Fortunately, Burns night comes on the 25 January, making it impossible for normal people to resist having a dram to toast the 'immortal memory'. However, the first three weeks can be a gloomy time, what with the weather and all, so I advise my foreign friends never to visit Scotland during that time.

Apart from Hogmanay and Burns night whisky has many other important social functions. At weddings, where people are supposed to be ecstatically happy, whisky is the fire in the hand that forges lasting bonds on the anvil of matrimony. It also has a life-giving vigour which is the natural expression of the community's hopes for the couple on their wedding night. (A secondary role at weddings is to give the over-enthusiastic piper something else to do with his hands).

At funerals, where people are supposed to be sad, whisky is the liquid mirror on which shared memories float, and the sedative that steadies the shaking hand.

Thus is whisky the most versatile of drinks in any social occasion. The appropriateness of whisky for either sad or happy outcomes, is of course why it is the drink of choice for those attending important rugby matches. (The situation does not arise for football, as soccer fans tend to drink lager, and have therefore long-since disgraced themselves and lost their right to take anything alcoholic into matches).

Every social situation that has a commemoration, a celebration or a right of passage, from birthdays to graduations, from promotions to retirement and from sporting victories to wetting the baby's head, whisky is the obvious drink to mark the occasion. Special bottlings or vintages can only enhance this role. (The spraying around of champagne has never really caught on in Scotland. It is not so much the choice of champagne as the waste of it that seems to be the problem).

It is still the celebration of Hogmanay and the Burns Supper that really show whisky in it most glowing social light. At Hogmanay (much more important to the Scots than Christmas) whisky is the warmth to protect us when travelling around in the cold. It is also wonderfully portable, slipping into coat pocket and handbag the way that boxes of wine and cases of Mexican beer just don't. It is the currency of first-footing. It is the natural choice to celebrate the turning of the year, with it's own inherent maturity and ability to wear a sad or a happy face and to look either forward or back. With a good single malt in your hand you can say 'here's tae us, wha's like us' with pride and impunity and even the feeling of being hung-over is nothing to be ashamed of when it is a collective thing shared with the rest of the nation.

By the time 25 January comes round a large part of the nation has a raging thirst and the Burns Supper provides the perfect excuse. Burns wrote with knowledge and passion on the subject of whisky. He was an exciseman and the popular stereotype is one in which the excisemen are soulless, emotionless creatures with no spark, no humour, no poetry, no joie de vivre, no elan vital, no savior faire, no French... Burns, of course, was the exact opposite, and while that fact did nothing to save the profession from the collective ill-will, it was more than enough to save Burns from any speck of contamination. Indeed, perhaps the reverence in which Burns is held owes something to the contradictions found in his life and work. Scotland always loves a lad o' pairts.

The dram also plays a central part in the ritual of the Burns Supper. The weather has something to do with it. I was once at a Burns Supper in July in the Signet Library in Edinburgh. Malt whisky was on the tables along with the salt and pepper and it just didn't feel right. Hot summer nights are thirsty, whereas in the middle of winter you hold the dram in your hand as if to extract something of the warming glow, you savour it, you enjoy the aroma and you hold on to a drop for the toast. That night in Edinburgh I saw a certain songwriter from Dundee somersaulting down the stairs of the Signet Library. Burns would never have done that (but then he wasn't from Dundee).

It is important that there should be a generous succession of speeches and toasts at a Burns Supper, the immortal memory, the toast to the lassies and the reply from the lassies. This is why those few organisations that still anachronistically exclude women feel the need to import one for the Burns Supper. These are simply an excuse for the measured and ritual consumption of whisky. In fact even before the speeches there is an important ritual, where the piper and the chef, having deliv-ered the haggis, are rewarded with a dram. The normal thing is for these players to knock back the *dram in one. This is something that both professions have considerable training in and is not recommended for normal folk at home (unless blended whisky is all that's available, in which case holding the nose at the same time is a good idea). The audience watches this ritual with glee, an energising frison of anticipation running through their veins and over their top lips. This is an important prelude to a successful night. These days whisky is often also used to anoint the haggis on the plate – not just a ritual libation, but a useful moistener for haggis that may have become dry from too much time in the bain-marie.*

Burns tends to overshadow other literary figures in Scotland. I intend to develop the concept of a Stevenson supper. His birthday being 13 November comes at a useful point in the year and there is enough in his work to build ritual around, including something to do with heather ale and atholl brose!

Throughout the world whisky has become a byword for hospitality. At home and in other countries I have been welcomed with a dram, sometimes in the traditional quaich, and a welcome is always the warmer for it. Long may it continue to lubricate countless moments of human warmth and togetherness.

The Tinkler's Waddin'

WILLIAM WATT (1792-1859)

In June, when broom in bloom was seen, and bracken waved fu' fresh and green,
And warm the sun, wi' silver sheen, the hills and glens did gladden, O.
Ae day, upon the Border bent, the tinklers pitched their gipsy tent,
And auld and young, wi' ae consent, resolved to haud a waddin, O.

Dirum a doo a doo a day, dirum a doo a daddie-o.
Dirrum a doo a doo a day, hurrah for the tinklers waddin' o.

The bridegroom was wild Norman Scott, wha thrice had broke the nuptial knot,
And aince was sentenced to be shot for breach o' martial orders, O.
His gleesome joe was Madge McKell, a spaewife match for Nick himsel',
Wi' glamour, cantrip, charm and spell, she frichted baith the Borders, O.

Dirum a doo, &c.

Nae priest was there wi' solemn face, nae clerk to claim o crowns the brace;
The piper and fiddler played the grace to set their gabs a steerin', O.
'Mang beef and mutton, pork and veal, 'mang paunches, plucks and fresh cow-heel,
Fat haggises and cauler jeel, they clawed awa' careerin', O.

Dirum a doo, &c.

Fresh salmon, newly ta'en in Tweed, saut ling and cod o' Shetland breed,
They worried, till kytes were like to screed, 'mang flagons and flasks o' gravy, O.
There was raisin kail and sweet-milk saps, and ewe-milk cheese in whangs and flaps,
And they rookit, to gust their gabs and craps, richt mony a cadger's cavie, O.

Dirum a doo, &c.

The drink flew round in wild galore, and some upraised a hideous roar;
Blythe Comus ne'er a queerer core saw seated round his table, O.
They drank, they danced, they swore, they sang, they quarrelled and 'greed the hale day lang,
And the wranglin' that rang amang the thrang wad match the tongues o' Babel, O.

Dirum a doo, &c.

The drink gaed doon before their drooth, that vexed baith mony a maw and mooth;
It dampit the fire o' age and youth, and every breist did sadden, O,
Till three stout loons flew owre the fell, at risk o' life, their drooth tae quell,
And robbed a neebourin' smuggler's still, to carry on the waddin', O.

Dirum a doo, &c.

Wi' thunderin shouts they hailed them back, to broach the barrels they werena slack,
While the fiddler's plane-tree leg they brak for playin' 'Fareweel to Whisky', O.
Delirium seized the 'roarious thrang, the bagpipes in the fire they flang,
And sowtherin' airns on riggins rang, the drink played siccan a pliskey, O.

Dirum a doo, &c.

The sun fell laigh owre Solway banks, while on they plied their roughsome pranks,
And the stalwart shadows o their shanks wide owre the muir were spreadin', O,
Till, heids and thraws, amang the whins, they fell wi' broken brows and shins,
And sair craist banes filled mony skins, to close the tinkler's waddin', O.

When I was a bairn my grandfather would dandle me on his knee singing 'Rothsay-O'. The original song to use that old strathspey tune was the Tinkler's Waddin'. In its day it was a very popular and widely sung song.

Whisky, of course, is the drink of choice for the many toasts at any Scottish wedding and the travellers or tinklers would always do social events with greater gusto than other folk. I once found myself in the midst of a Bachannalian riot in the Wicklow Mountains, which my Dublin friend assured me was 'a knackers' wedding', and I can vouch for their gusto and abandon.

The wedding feast running out of drink echoes the story told in 'The Wedding at Cana' but in the absence of anyone able to perform miracles, robbing 'a neebourin' smuggler's still' would do the job just as well.

William Watt came from West Linton but lived most of his life in East Kilbride. He also wrote 'Kate Dalrymple'.

The Wedding of Shon MacLean

ROBERT BUCHANAN (1841-1901)

To the wedding of Shon Maclean
Twenty pipers together
Came in the wind and the rain
Playing across the heather;
Backward their ribbons flew
Blast upon blast they blew
Each clad in tartan new,
Bonnet and blackcock feather;
And every piper was fou,
Twenty pipers together!

At the wedding of Shon Maclean
They blew with lungs of leather,
And blythesome was the strain
Those pipers played together!
Moist with the mountain-dew,
Mighty of bone and thew,
Each with the bonnet of blue
Tartan and blackcock feather;
And every piper was fou,
Twenty pipers together!

At the wedding of Shon Maclean,
Twenty pipers together,
They blew with might and main,
Through wonderful lungs of leather!
Wild was the hullabaloo!
They stamped, they screamed, they crew!
Twenty strong blasts they blew,
Holding the heart in tether;
And every piper was fou,
Twenty pipers together!

The small stars twinkled over the heather,
As the pipers wandered away together,
But one by one on the journey dropt,
Clutching his pipes, and there he stopt!
One by one on the dark hillside
Each faint blast of the bagpipes died,
Amid the wind and the rain!
And the twenty pipers at break of day
In twenty different bogholes lay,
Serenely sleeping upon their way
From the wedding of Shon Maclean.

Pipers have many occupational hazards, red faces from sustained, hard blowing, white knees from the cold wind, and liver problems from consumption of the obligatory drams which are thrust into their hands at weddings, Burns Suppers and other such occasions. Naturally, they are expected to knock back these drams in one go – to show how manly they are. Of course if they didn't wear skirts all the time, they might not have to prove the point so frequently.

Christmas Cheer

PATRICK TAYLOR

The fire that fills the grain
Distilled to amber, in a glass,
Will stand decanted once again
As Christmas comes to pass.

The whisky should be aged
And not just one that passes,
With proper reverence uncaged
And drunk from proper glasses.

A lead cut glass with weight
And finely scooped, will be required;
A mind that's in the proper state
Of calm - alert, not tired.

(For pick-me-ups use gin)
The fingers should be dry, to slip
Along a smooth cut edge. Begin
By moistening the lip

To glide around the rim;
Rotate the glass to glint in light
Of glowing coals, while lamps are dim,
For whisky drunk by night

Is best, when tales of old
Come tumbling out by dint of grain
And as familiar yarns are told
Decanters tilt again!

This poem is a kind of instruction on how to appreciate whisky – or is it an instruction on how to appreciate Christmas? In either case, the important bit is in the last verse.

Hogmanay

NORMAN MacCAIG (1910-1996)

Murdo gave the cock meal
damped with whisky. It stood
on tiptoe, crowed eight times
and fell flat on its beak.

Later, Murdo, after the fifth verse
of *The Isle of Mull*,
fell, glass in hand,
flat on his back - doing in six hours
what the cock had done
in two minutes.

I was there. And now I see
the cock crowing with Murdo's face
and Murdo's wings flapping
as down he went.

It was a long way home.

*I am reminded of a wee poem translated
from the Gaelic in an old issue of Tocher
magazine.
'This New Year is not like any other
I'm missing those that are away.
Only a dog and a cat for company -
I got them both drunk.'*

*How sad to be alone at Hogmanay. At least
with whisky you need never be completely
alone.*

Song: The Steeple Bar, Perth

SYDNEY GOODSIR SMITH (1915-1975)

O it's dowf tae be drinkin alane, my luve,
When I wud drink wi my dear,
Nor Crabbie nor Bell's can fire me, luve,
As they wud an you were here.

O I'd drink wi us aa again, my luve,
As we aa did yester year,
But me buckos 're scattered afar, my luve,
An I greit intil my beer.

Wi' my third I'll drink tae oor Denis, luve,
My fourth great John's, the bauld an steir,
My fifth, auld Hector, the rebelly carle,
An my sixth tae oorsels, my dear.

And noo I've forgot dear Bonz the mad –
Wud the Pawky Duke were near,
So he'll hae the seeventh, the darlin lad,
And again tae oorsels, my dear.

My brains 're fleein, I cannae think
O' the dizzen ithers I wud were here;
Tae Maury the neist wee Bell's I'll drink,
Tae Dauvit a pint – an I'm sunk – gey near.

O I'm gettin a wee thing fou, my luve,
An donnert an like tae fleer –
For, jeez, it's dreich tae get pissed, my luve,
Wi nane o' my looed yins here.

*A number of Sydney Goodsir Smith's poems
are called 'song' or 'sang', but I have no
evidence of a tune for this. It is a wonderful
picture of whisky working as a comfort and
consolation for the lonely, while at the same
time hinting at its ability to evoke the past.
There is no doubt that whisky is at its most
powerful when cementing the bond of
friendship in real company – which is why
this poem, showing the opposite picture,
works so well.*

An Abacus o' Decay

RAYMOND VITTESSE

He's skailt on the bar's formica bleck
a puckle gowden draps o whisky.

Whaur is the strength that fund
gowden hairst in driechest grund?

The men sat lauchin here,
dealt cairds, scrabbelt bones,
cried oot for luck an' mair beer,
mairched oot o the ploo chains
and intil the war...

Horses claitter doon cobbelt streets.

Shops, wi ham-strung rafters,
smell o bacon, o new-cut cheese.

The lads f'ae the Mairt,
wi sharn on their feet,
birl aboot the howff sawins,
(Tam on the moothie
Peem on the spoons),
heechin, skirlin, lowpin, fleein,
faain doon,

      stotterin hame...

Whaur's the real warl gane?

On the bar's formica bleck
a puckle gowden draps o whisky
are coontin the time, coontin
the time: an abacus o decay.

The dreepin gless quavers
at thin cauld lips.

Furious music batters out
American dreams.

He hirples back tae his far-awa neuk.

The affable, shining, hawk-eyed young
    barman
darts over, swoops down, wipes clean.

Raymond Vittesse's powerful imagery turns the whisky glass into a crystal or a pool through which the past (with its happier social times) looms, clears, fades and disappears with great emotional impact.

The Bottle

ROBERT BUCHANAN SMITH

The bottle, virginal,
Waited the attention, admiration
And affection of the three.

From the first lip-licking glass,
They savoured slowly forty years
Of blended yesterdays,

Maturing friendships, proof
Against old age, or absence, death
Was a detail not worth mentioning.

When there was little left in the bottle,
Three sat silent, fumbling
With the loose change of their thoughts.

The talking done, two rose for the
Broad road home, feet high at the kerbs.
The third found half a glass remained,

Sat for an hour with it,
And wrote a poem.
The bottle was a whore, discarded.

Continuing the theme of whisky as a link with the past, this poem captures the comradeship of men and the almost sexual appreciation of a good dram.

Willie Brewed a Peck o' Maut

ROBERT BURNS (1759-1796)

O, Willie brewed a peck o' maut,
And Rob and Allan cam' to prie;
Three blyther hearts that lea-lang nicht
Ye wadna find in Christendie.

We are na fou, we're nae that fou,
But just a drappie in oor e'e!
The cock may craw, the day may daw',
But aye we'll taste the barley bree.

Here are we met, three merry boys,
Three merry boys I trow are we;
And mony's the nicht we've merry been,
And mony mair we hope to be!

We are na fou, &c.

It is the moon, I ken her horn,
That's blinkin' in the lift sae hie:
She shines sae bright tae wyle us hame,
But, by my sooth, she'll wait a wee!

We are na fou, &c.

Wha first shall rise to gang awa,
A cuckold, coward loon is he!
Wha first beside his chair shall fa',
He is the King amang us three!

We are na fou, &c.

I've heard some people say that this song is about beer, not whisky. Certainly all the words used are slightly ambiguous. 'Drappie' and 'barley bree' suggest whisky but could be beer and 'brewed' suggests beer but could be whisky (see e. g. 'O What a Parish'). For the moment I choose to interpret it as whisky, and delight in the ironic image of an exciseman (Burns) enjoying a wee drop of home-made whisky with his two friends Willie Nicol and Allan Masterton. (The tune was said to be composed by Masterton).

Actually, the last verse shows that the evening turned into a drinking contest – the rules being that the first one to leave is a coward and a cuckold while the first one to collapse unconscious is the winner! Yet again Burns captures something quintessentially Scottish in our approach to drink.

Wee Draps an' Often

JAMES NEILSON (1844-1883)

The Laird Macintosh has mair sense than
  be saucy,
An' aft at the smiddy, whaur labour loud
  rings,
He ca's on young Vulcan, wha sweats sae an'
  blaws sae,
An' tells him the drappie gies pith to his
  swings;
Then doun in frien' Nanny's the Whig and
  the Tory
May wrangle ower ilk ane's political creed,
An' say things far mair to their shame than
  their glory-
But ower the bit drappie they're ever
  agreed.

Oh, wee draps an' often – ay, wee draps an' often –
It's fair to get frisky, but foul to get fou;
Wee drappies an' waste na; jist aye a bit taste na,
An' aye a bit sixpence the stoup to renew.

Wi' business in ae haun', the glass in the
  ither,
They aiblins sit hours ower the price o' a
  job;
They reckon, and taste then – then reckon,
  an' swither
Gin ane wants to cheat, or the ither to rob;
An' gossips mourn ower the example
  they're settin',
An' grudge to auld Nanny the bite for her
  mou';
But, faith, their example is worth ne'er for-
  gettin',
When baith come out hearty an' nane o'
  them fu'.

Oh, wee draps an' often, &c.

The twasome then part, aye the best o' guid
  fellows,
The glance o' guid-nature illumines ilk e'e;
The smith wi' renewed strength brings
  roars frae his bellows,
An' systems o' wee stars his hammer make
  flee.
The laird, noo sae vogie, gaes joggin' the
  lichter,
An' blither an' fresher returns to his hame.
It's wee draps mak' whilocks o' lifetime the
  brichter,
If a' were content wi' jist wee draps the
  same.

Oh, wee draps an' often, &c.

James Neilson was a member of the Glasgow Ballad Club. The Laird and the blacksmith conclude their business deal with a wee dram and not only do they part contented and on best of terms, but the smith has recharged his physical strength. Great stuff this whisky!

Lochanside

JIM MALCOLM

Come the winter, cauld and dreary
Brings the hawk doon frae the high scree
Tae the whin whaur snawy hares hide
A' aroond the Lochanside.

Come the spring the land lies weary
Till the sun shines oot sae cheery
Brings the bloom for a' o' June's pride
A' aroond the Lochanside.

If you'd been you'd have seen the scatter
O' the peezies o'er the machair
When abune, the tawny owl glides
A' aroond the Lochanside

And the heron, he comes a-creepin'
Through the rashes sae green and dreepin'
To the pool whaur wily troot slide
A' aroond the Lochanside.

Aye if you ever ha'e a reason
Tae be here in ony season
Come and try the barley bree in
Roond the fire on Lochanside.

Simmer time the fish are loupin'
Dippers in the burnies coupin'
Swallaes flee from dawn til e'en-tide
A' aroond the Lochanside.
By the autumn the pinks are winging
Blaeb'rries o'er the moors are hinging
Salmon through the surging spate fight
A' aroond the Lochanside

If you'd been you'd have seen the scatter
O' the peezies o'er the machair
When abune, the tawny owl glides
A' aroond the Lochanside

And the heron, he comes a-creepin'
Through the rashes sae green and dreepin'
Tae the pool where wily troot slide
A' aroond the Lochanside.

Aye if you ever ha'e a reason
Tae be here in ony season
Come and try the barley bree in
Roond the fire on Lochanside.

Aye if you ever ha'e a notion
Tae be welcomed wi' devotion
Traivel home o'er ony ocean
Tae be here on Lochanside.

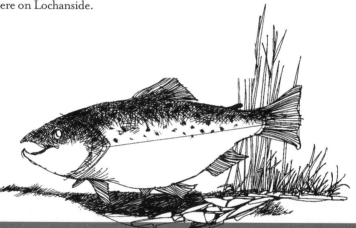

Jim Malcolm has used John McLellan's lovely pipe tune to create a song that evokes a scene familiar and dear to his angler's heart. The appreciation of nature in the wild is palpable and the notion of friends sharing a dram in the summer gloaming by a hill loch is hard to resist. Incidentally a smear of whisky on the skin can be effective in keeping off the midges – perhaps the only imaginable external use of whisky – it doesn't actually deter the midge because they love it as well, but it slows down their reaction time so you can swot them much more efficiently. The anaesthetic effect is also valuable (for you, that is, not the midge).

The song can be found on Jim's CD 'Resonance'.

Happy We Are A' Thegither

TRADITIONAL

Here around the ingle bleezin',
Wha sae happy and sae free?
Tho' the northern wind blaws freezin',
Frien'ship warms baith you and me.

Happy we are a' thegither,
Happy we'll be, ane an' a';
Time shall see us a' the blyther
Ere we rise to gang awa.

See the miser o'er his treasure
Gloatin' wi' a greedy e'e!
Can he feel the glow o' pleasure
That around us here we see?

Happy we are, &c.

Thus then let us a' be tassin'
Aff our stoups o' gen'rous flame;
And while roun' the board 'tis passin',
Raise a sang in frien'ship's name.

Happy we are, &c.

Frien'ship maks us a' mair happy,
Frien'ship gies us a' delight;
Frien'ship consecrates the drappie,
Frien'ship brings us here the night.

Happy we are, &c.

'Friendship consecrates the drappie' – and of course vice versa. It is no accident or surprise that whisky has become such an international symbol of friendship. Long may that continue.

A Wee Drappie o't

TRADITIONAL

This life is a journey we a' hae to gang,
And care is the burden we carry alang;
Though heavy be the burden and poverty
   our lot,
We'll be happy a' thegither owre a wee
   drappie o't.

Owre a wee drappie o't, owre a wee drappie o't
We'll be happy a' thegither owre a wee drappie o't.

View the birk in winter, a' leafless and bare,
Resemblin' a man wi' a burden o' care,
But view the birk in summer, wi' its braw,
   leafy coat,
Rejoicin' like a man owre a wee drappie o't.

Owre a wee drappie o't, &c.

We're a' met thegither owre a glass and a
   sang,
We're a' met thegither by special command;
Free frae mean ambition and every evil
   thought,
We'll be happy while we may owre a wee
   drappie o't.

Owre a wee drappie o't, &c.

When friendship and truth and gude fel-
   lowship reign,
And fouk grown auld are made youthfu'
   again;
Where ilka heart is happy, and warldly cares
   forgot,
Is when we're met thegither owre a wee
   drappie o't.

Owre a wee drappie o't, &c.

Job in his lamentation said man was made
   tae mourn,
That there's nae such thing as pleasure frae
   the cradle to the urn;
But in his meditation Job shurely had for-
   got,
The pleasure man derives owre a wee drap-
   pie o't.

Owre a wee drappie o't, &c.

This is basically the version from Ford's 'Vagabong Songs and Ballads'. There are many others, both shorter and longer. In a life of toil and care, moments of pleasure can be rare, but with a wee dram to help things along they can be heart-warming and memorable.

A Golden Wine in the Gaidhealtachd

(To W. D. MacColl and our hosts and hostesses in Arisaig, Eigg, South Uist, Raasay, Skye, Barra and Mull)

HUGH MacDIARMID (1892-1978)

In Scotland in the Gaidhealtachd there's a gold-
en wine
Still to be found in a few houses here and there
Where the secret of it's making has been kept for
centuries
- Nor would it avail to steal the secret, since it
cannot be made elsewhere.

In Scotland in the Gaidhealtachd there's a gold-
en wine
Carelessly and irreligiously quaffed it might be
taken
For a very fine Champagne. But it is not an
effervescing wine
Although its delicate piquancy produces a some-
what similar effect upon the palate.

In Scotland in the Gaidhealtachd there's a gold-
en wine,
A wine that demands so deliberate a pause,
In order to detect its hidden peculiarities
And subtle exquisiteness of its flavour, that to
drink it
Is really more a moral than a physical delight.
There is a deliciousness in it that eludes analysis
And like whatever else is superlatively good
Is better appreciated by the memory
Than by present consciousness.

In Scotland in the Gaidhealtachd there's a gold-
en wine.
One of its most ethereal charms lies
In the transitory life of its richest qualities,
For while it requires a certain leisure and delay
Yet if you linger too long upon the draught it
becomes
Disenchanted both of its fragrance and its
flavour.

In Scotland in the Gaidhealtachd there's a gold-
en wine.
The lustre should not be forgotten among the
other
Admirable embodiments of this rare wine; for,
as it stands in a glass
A little circle of light glows round about it,
The finest Orvieto or that famous wine,
The Est Est Est of Montefiascone
Is vulgar in comparison. This is surely
The wine of the Golden Age such as Bacchus
himself
First taught mankind to press from the choicest
of his grapes.

In Scotland in the Gaidhealtachd there's a golden wine.
There is a tradition that if any of it were sent to market
This wine would lose all its wonderful qualities.
Not a drop of it therefore has ever been sold,
Or ever will be. Indeed the wine is so fond
Of its native home that a transportation
Of even a few miles turns it quite sour.
Yet the custom of those who have it has always been and still is
To let it flow freely whenever those
Whom they love and honour sit at the board
But it cannot be drunk in all the world
Save under these particular roofs in Arisaig and Eigg.

In Tobermory, South Uist, Barra, Raasay and Skye,
Nor can they see or smell or taste it who are not
Competent receivers - nor could they bestow
Who lack the sense of operative form - this consecrated juice
Symbolising the holy virtues of hospitality and social kindness.

Through what else can Scotland recover its poise
Save, as Very Hope believes, this golden wine yet?

This poem is in English rather than Scots, which is slightly unusual for MacDiarmid. It may be an early work, but because the subject is mainly Gaelic, the English language suits it well. Given the inexorable link between whisky and hospitality the 'golden wine' is at the very least an allusion to whisky, though it is obviously intended to be something wider and greater - a spiritual essence of human hospitality.

Tak' a Dram

IAN SINCLAIR

Oh, this evening's passed so quickly,
And the music's almost done;
We've heard the piper and the fiddler,
The singer and his song.
The time has come for us to leave you;
One last song before we go;
So button up and aye be cheery
Tak a dram afore ye go.
Button up and aye be cheery,
Tak a dram afore ye go.

For this night we will remember,
And the music's been just fine;
But the cold, grey land of Caithness
Can be cruel and unkind.
We must bid fareweel and leave you;
Travel through the ice and snow;
So button up, &c.

So goodnight and God be with you
And watch over you until
We can a' meet here thegither,
And our glasses we will refill.
We'll drink a health tae absent friends
And make the beer and whisky flow,
So button up, &c.

Ian Sinclair comes from Caithness where whisky is a necessary form of central heating. The Scots always seem reluctant to stop when they're having a social get together (especially when there's a dram involved). I can't decide if that's because joyous occasions are so rare or because of our natural gregarious glee or whether it's actually the whisky that we don't want to give up.

Just a Wee Deoch an Dorus

R.F. MORRISON and WHIT CUNCLIFFE

There's a good old Scottish custom
That has stood the test o' time;
Its a custom that's been carried out
In every land and clime.
Wherever Scots are gathered
It's aye the usual thing,
Just before we say goodnight,
We raise our cups and sing –

I like a man, that is a man,
A man that's straight and fair.
A sort of man who will and can,
In all things do his share.
I like a man, a jolly man,
The sort of man you know
The kind of chap that slaps your back
And says 'before you go'.

Just a wee deoch and dorus,
Just a wee yin that's a'
Just a wee deoch and doris,
Afore we gang awa'.
There's a wee wifie waitin'
In a wee butt and ben;
If you can say 'its a braw, bricht,
Moonlicht nicht'
Well you're a' richt, ye ken.

Just a wee deoch and dorus, &c.

'Deoch an dorus' is Gaelic for a health at the door. My grandfather (Papa Jock Ireland) used to sing this old music hall song and it was a long time before I realised that it wasn't about a couple called Jock and Doris.

One more for the road – one more drink, one more song, one more dance – is very much a Scottish custom that can make any informal gathering into an all-nighter. We hate the sound of instrument case being shut, the sound of the stopper being put in the bottle, the sound of the latch on the gate, and the sound of the book being closed at the end of the day…

TUNES

1. More Than Just a Dram (Robin Laing)

Verse

Chorus

2. John Barleycorn (Robin Laing)

3. A Bottle o' the Best (Jack Foley)

4. Our Glens (George Donald)

5. Whisky Johnny (trad.)

6. Here's to You Again *and* When Johnnie was Gi'en to the Weetin' his Mou' (trad. *Toddlin' Hame*)

Verse

Chorus

7. Campbeltown Loch (Andy Stewart)

Chorus

Verse

8. A Wee Drap o' Whisky (trad.)

9. What a Mischief Whisky's Done (trad.)

193

10. Tee-total Song (trad. *Willie Wabster*)

11. The Barley Bree (trad. *There's nae Luck Aboot the Hoose*)

12. Nancy's Whisky (trad.)

Verse

Chorus

13. John Barleycorn my Jo (trad. *John Anderson*)

14. Piper MacNeil (trad.)

15. Cripple Kirsty (trad. *Maggie Lauder*)

16. The Heilan' Hills (trad.)

17. Neil Gow's Fareweel to Whisky *and* Donal' Don (Neil Gow)

18. A Cogie o' Yill (Andrew Sheriffs)

19. The Queer Folk i' the Shaws (James Fisher)

20. Alan MacLean (trad.)

21. Jock Geddes and the Soo (trad. *Roy's Wife o' Aldivalloch*)

Verse

Chorus

22. The Gulls o' Invergordon, The Battle of Corriemuckloch *and* The Tinkler's Waddin' (trad.)

23. The Ghost wi' the Squeaky Wheel (Tom Clelland)

24. The Best o' the Barley (Brian McNeill)

25. Three Men Frae Overton (Billy Stewart)

196

26. The Devil Uisge Beatha (Alan Reid)

27. Oh What a Parish (trad. *Over the Water to Charlie*)

28. Twelve and a Tanner a Bottle (Will Fyffe)

29. The De'ils Awa' wi' th' Exciseman (trad.)

197

30. The Exciseman in a Coal Pit (trad.)

31. Shining Clear (Alan Reid)

32. The Ewie wi' the Crookit Horn (trad.)

33. Tak' It, Man, Tak' It (David Webster)

34. Bung Your Eye (trad.)

35. Donal' Blue (trad.)

36. Drap o' Capie-O (trad.)

37. The Wee Wifikie (Dr Alexander Geddes)

38. Tall Tale (trad. *The Roving Journeyman*)

39. The Wag at the Wa' (trad.)

40. Johnny My Man (trad.)

41. Willie Brew'd a Peck o' Maut (Allan Masterton)

42. Lochanside (John McLellan)

43. Happy We Are A' Thegither (trad.)

44. A Wee Drappie o't (trad.)

45. Tak' a Dram (Ian Sinclair)

46. Just a Wee Deoch an' Dorus (Whit Cunliffe)

abune - above
aft - often
ahint - behind
aiblins - perhaps, possibly
ain - own
airls - a deposit as earnest of more to come
airn - iron
amo' - among
aneath - beneath
atweel - indeed, of course
auldfarran - old fashioned
ava - at all
awnie - bearded
ayont - beyond
b'roo - welfare
bachals - slippers, down-at-heel shoes
banie - big-boned, stout
bauld - bold
bawbee - halfpenny
bear - barley
bee-skep - beehive
begoud - began
bein/bien - thriving, comfortable
ben - hill
besom - slovenly woman
bicker - beaker
bide - to stay
bield - shelter
biggit - built
billie - brother, comrade
binna - be not
birl - to spin
bittock - a little bit, a short distance
blanter - oats
blate - shy, bashful
blather - bladder
bleeze - blaze
blue - whisky
bodach - an old man
bonnock - cake, bannock
bousing - drinking
brash - short, severe bout of illness
braw - fine, handsome
breared - sprouted
bree/broe - liquor, whisky, brew
breeks - trousers
brock - badger
broo - brow
brose - porridge, oatmeal mixed with some liquid
brunstane - brimstone

brust - burst
bubbly-jock - turkey cock
bum - to hum
burn - brook
burnewin - blacksmith
buss - bush
bussle - bustle
but and ben - two-roomed cottage, kitchen and parlour
by my sooth - believe me
ca' - to knock
cadger - itinerant dealer
cadgy - gay, wanton, in good spirits
cantrip - magic spell
canty - pleasant, cheerful
cap'stane - cope stone
capie/cappie - drinking cup, beer
carl/carle - man
carline/carling - old woman
cauldrife - cold, chilly
cauler - fresh
cavie - hen-coop
chackit - checked
change-house - ale-house, tavern
chaunt - to sing
chaup - knock, blow
chauved - paled
cheek-for-chow - side by side
cheel/chiel - fellow
cheer - chair
chuffie - fat, chubby of cheek
clack - noisy talk
claes - clothes
claith - cloth
clapper - sharp, rattling noise
clappertie-clink - the sound of a mill clapper
claucht - a clutch, grasp
clishmaclavers - idle talk, gossip
clorty - dirty, messy
cockauds - cockades
cogie - a small wooden vessel
confab - confabulation
cood - cud
coothie - pleasant, kind
copt - caught
core - company
cottar - inhabitant of a cot house or cottage
coup - to capsize, to drink off
cow the cadie - to outdo, surpass
crabbit - bad-tempered

crack - conversation, tales
craig/craigie - throat
craist - shattered
crankous - fretful, captious
cranky - irritable
crap - a bird's crop, throat
craps - crops
cratur - creature, whisky
creeshy - greasy, fat
creish - to thrash, beat
crippen - shrivelled
crouse - cheerful
cuffet - blow
cuif - simpleton, fool
cunyie - money, coin
cuttie - short
dagonit - an expletive, confound it
dams - urine
dauner - to stroll, saunter
deave - to deafen
deen - done
deoch an dorus - a drink or health at the door,
dicht - to wipe
dinsome - noisy
disjaskit - forlorn, dejected
divor - debtor, rogue
doited - foolish
donnart - stupefied, stunned
dorty - proud, haughty
douce - gentle
dour - stern, sullen
dowf - melancholy, gloomy
dowie - sad, mournful
doylt - dazed, muddled, blundering along
dram-shop - public house
drap/drappie - drop, drink
dree - to endure, suffer
dreich - tedious, dull, wearisome
drone - the lowest boy in the class
drouth - thirst
drucken - drunk
dub - a puddle
dung - smashed
dunt - a blow, a knock
dwalling - dwelling
dwam - swoon
dwine/dwyne - waste away
dyke - wall
dyster - dyer
een - eyes
eerie - apprehensive, afraid
enow - enough
ettle - to intend
eidently - diligently, attentively

ewie - ewe
fae - foe
fae/frae - from
fain - eager, anxious
fan - when
fand - found
fang - the power of suction in a pump
fash - trouble
fat/fit - what
feg - a thing of no value, a fig
fen' - to defend, manage to subsist
fess - to fetch
fidge - to fidget
fit - foot
flair - floor
fleer - to whimper
fley - to frighten
flite/flyte - to scold
flow - a small quantity of meal
forrit - forward
fou' - full, drunk
fouk - folk, people
foul fa' - devil take! evil befall!
foumart - polecat
freath - to froth or foam
freen - friend
frichtit - frightened
froon - frown
fuddle - drinking bout
fushonless - tasteless, feeble
fyle - soil, defile, befoul
gab - to talk entertainingly
gang - go
gar - to make
gauger - exciseman
gaun - going
gauntet - yawned
gavil - gable, wide open door
gean - cherry tree
gey'n - considerably
gill-stoup - drinking vessel holding a gill
girn - to grimace
glabber - liquid mud
Glaisca - Glasgow
glar/glaur - mud
gleg - clever, bright
glib-gabbed - fluent, talkative
glimmer - blink
glock - to gurgle
gloom - frown
glunch - sour look or frown
gowden - golden
gowk - cuckoo, foolish person
graith - harness for horses

grane – groan
gruntle – snout or face
guidman – master of the house, husband
gust – to please the palate
gusty – pleasing the palate
gweed – good
hairst – harvest
haith! – exclamation of surprise
hale – whole, sound
hallen – partition wall between door and fireplace
halt – defective
hantle – a large quantity
harl – drag, haul
harns – brains
hash – mess, muddle, blockhead
haud – to hold
hauf – half, whisky
haugh – level ground beside a stream
haun – hand
havers – nonsense, foolish talk
heich – in high spirits
het pint – drink of ale and spirits drunk on new year's eve
hil't – held, raised
hinny – honey
hoast – cough
hodden-grey – grey homespun woollen cloth
hoo – how
horn – drinking vessel, draught of liquor
hotch-potch – medley, confused jumble
howdie – midwife
howff – residence, tavern
hurl – a lift
ilk/ilka – each
ingle – fireplace, hearth
jalouse – to suspect, guess, imagine
jaud – a jade
jaw – splash of water
jeel – jelly
jink – to dodge
jo/joe – sweetheart
jouk – to duck, avoid
kae – jackdaw, thievish or mischievous person
kail – green vegetables
keel – any marking substance
ken – to know
kent – knew
kink-hoast – whooping-cough
kintra – country
kir – cheerful, wanton
kist – chest
kitchen – to season
knag – knob, peg
kyte – stomach

kythe – to show, become known
laigh – low
lampin' – striding
lap – did leap
lauchin' – laughing
lear – learning
leeze me on – an expression of pleasure
libbit – castrated, gelded
lift – the sky
lilt – to sing
limmers – rascals, prostitutes
lippen – to trust, depend upon
loof – palm of hand
loon – fellow, rascal
lounder – to beat severely
loup – to jump, leap
louse – to loosen, let free
lowe – flame, fire
lucky – wife
lug – ear
lug – to carry
lum – chimney
machair – sandy tract by the sea
mae – more
Mahoun – name for the devil
mashlum – mixed grain
massy – mossy
maudlin – tipsy
maun – must
mauna – must not
maut – malt
mishanter – misfortune
mixtie-maxtie – confused, jumbled
moo/mou' – mouth
muckle – large, great
mutchkin – liquid measure equal to an english pint
muter – multure
ne'er-dae-weel – foolhardy
neb – nose
neeps – turnips
neist – next
neive – fist
neivefu' – handful
new'r day – new year's day
nickum – mischievous boy
noddle – head
ocht – aught, anything
pad – to go on foot
parritch – porridge
pat – pot
pawkie – shrewd, sly
peezie – lapwing
pickle – a small quantity
pin – stopper

pine - pain
plack - small copper coin
plenish'd - furnished
plisky' - trick, prank
ploo - plough
plough-pettle - plough-staff
plumper - plunger
plunker - a large marble
pock - bag, sack
poopit - pulpit
pooshin - poison
pow - forehead
pree/prie - to taste
prounach - splinters
puckle - a small quantity
puddock - frog
quat - to quit
quate - quiet
quod - prison
rape - rope
rauchle tongued - fearless, plain speaking
ream - to froth
red-wud - raging mad
reek - smoke
reenge the ribs - clear the bars of a grate
reeve - to split asunder
reiver - robber, freebooter
rickle o' banes - a living skeleton
riggin - head
rook - to plunder
rouch - rough, long-bearded
roupit - hoarse, spent with shouting
rout - rolled, twisted and turned
routh/rowth - plenty
row - to move around, fetch
rund - round
rung - cudgel, staff
sanct/saunt - saint
sark - shirt
sark-neck - shirt collar
saul - sold
sax - six
scaith - injury
scant - scarce
scart - to scratch
scawlin' - railing at, abusing
scrabbelt - puny
screech - to scream
screed - to tear
screigh of day - the dawn
scrieve - to glide quickly along
scunner - disgust
seen - soon
shanks - legs

shanks-naigs - on one's own legs
sharn - cow dung
sheel - to shovel
shiel' - to shelter
shoon - shoes
shouther - shoulder
shust - just
sic - such
siccan - such a
siller - silver
skailt - spilled
skeich - spirited, skittish
skelp - slap, smack
skirl - to scream, shriek
skite - to skate off, a blow delivered sideways
sklim - to climb
skoog/skook - to skulk, not to look one straight
in the face
slacken/slocken - to quench, slake
slae - sloe
slitter - slobber
smeeky - smoky
smo'er - smother
snuffy - sulky
soo - sow
soom - swim
soop - to sweep
soss - a mess
sough - whizzing sound
souter - shoemaker
southerin' airns - soldering irons
sowp - a sip, a drink
spae-wife - female fortune teller
sparra - sparrow
spean - to wean
spier - to ask
spindle-shanks - long thin legs
spunge - purse, fob
spunkie - lively, spirited
starns - stars
stauncher - to stagger
staw - a dislike, aversion
steek - to shut, fasten
steep - tub
steer/steir - to stir, cause to move
stell - whisky still
stoat/stott - to stagger
stot - a stupid, clumsy fellow
stoup/stowp - flagon, drinking vessel
stown - stolen
strae - straw
strae-death - natural death
straik - stroke
studdie - anvil

sucker - sugar
swains - sawdust
sweel - swill
sweir - lazy
swite - sweat
syne - ago, since
tait - a small quantity of anything
tapsalteer/tapsalteerie - topsy-turvy, upside down
targe - to beat, to discipline
tashed - soiled, damaged
tass - toss
teem - to pour
thole - to bear, suffer
thoomb - thumb
thrang - busy
thrapple - windpipe, neck
thraw - a twist
thretty - thirty
throu'ther - unmethodical, in a mess
tift - to quaff
tine - to lose
tipenny - twopenny
toddle - stagger
took - a sup
toom - empty
toon - town
trig - smart, neat
trow - to feel sure, to make one believe
trow - to toss liquid around in a vessel
tummlet - tumbled
tutie - a woman tippler
twal - twelve
twin - to separate
twines - bonds
tyke - dog, clownish fellow
tynd - lost

tyne - to lose, forfeit
unco - adv.- very, adj. - strange
vera - very
vogie - merry, cheerful
vrocht - wrought
wae - woe
wale - choice
wame - belly
wauket - hardened, calloused
waur - worse
wean/weanie - little child
weasan/wizen - windpipe
weeda - widow
weel-faured - good looking
weet - wet
weyd - weighed
whang - a lump, large piece or slice
wheen - a number, a quantity, a few
whiles - sometimes
whilock - a short space of time
whin - furze, gorse
whittrock - weasel
wicht - wight, fellow
wight - weight
wimple - to wind
winnock - window
wist - wished
woo'-wool
wrack - to torment
wud - angry
wycelike - wise
wyte - blame
yammer/yaummer - to talk loudly and incessantly
yill - ale
yirth - earth

INDEX OF SONGS AND POEMS

Some CDs by ROBIN LAING

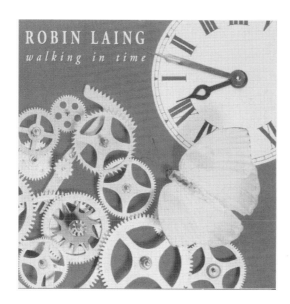

Walking in Time
(Greentrax 072)

*"Superior craftsmanship…
A very impressive album"*

THE SCOTSMAN

Edinburgh Skyline
(Greentrax 021)

*"Demonstrates clearly that he is a
major songwriting talent"*

EVENING NEWS

The Angels' Share
(Greentrax 137)

*"Robin Laing has few superiors.
He is heard at his compelling best in
'The Angels' Share'."*

THE SCOTSMAN

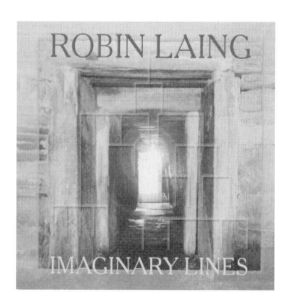

Imaginary Lines
(Greentrax 185)

*"Another first-rate collection by a
master of the genre"*

THE SCOTS MAGAZINE

Some other books published by **LUATH** PRESS

On the Trail of Robert Service

GW Lockhart

ISBN 0 946487 24 3 PBK £7.99

Robert Service is famed world-wide for his eye-witness verse-pictures of the Klondike goldrush. As a war poet, his work outsold Owen and Sassoon, and he went on to become the world's first million selling poet. In search of adventure and new experiences, he emigrated from Scotland to Canada in 1890 where he was caught up in the aftermath of the raging gold fever. His vivid dramatic verse bring to life the wild, larger than life characters of the gold rush Yukon, their bar-room brawls, their lust for gold, their trigger-happy gambles with life and love. 'The Shooting of Dan McGrew' is perhaps his most famous poem:

> A bunch of the boys were whooping it up in the Malamute saloon;
> The kid that handles the music box was hitting a ragtime tune;
> Back of the bar in a solo game, sat Dangerous Dan McGrew,
> And watching his luck was his light o'love, the lady that's known as Lou.

His storytelling powers have brought Robert Service enduring fame, particularly in North America and Scotland where he is something of a cult figure.

Starting in Scotland, *On the Trail of Robert Service* follows Service as he wanders through British Columbia, Oregon, California, Mexico, Cuba, Tahiti, Russia, Turkey and the Balkans, finally 'settling' in France.

This revised edition includes an expanded selection of illustrations of scenes from the Klondike as well as several photographs from the family of Robert Service on his travels around the world.

Wallace Lockhart, an expert on Scottish traditional folk music and dance, is the author of *Highland Balls & Village Halls* and *Fiddles & Folk*. His relish for a well-told tale in popular vernacular led him to fall in love with the verse of Robert Service and write his biography.

'*A fitting tribute to a remarkable man - a bank clerk who wanted to become a cowboy. It is hard to imagine a bank clerk writing such lines as:*

> *A bunch of boys were whooping it up...*

The income from his writing actually exceeded his bank salary by a factor of five and he resigned to pursue a full time writing career.' Charles Munn,
THE SCOTTISH BANKER

'*Robert Service claimed he wrote for those who wouldn't be seen dead reading poetry. His was an almost unbelievably mobile life... Lockhart hangs on breathlessly, enthusiastically unearthing clues to the poet's life.*' Ruth Thomas,
SCOTTISH BOOK COLLECTOR

'*This enthralling biography will delight Service lovers in both the Old World and the New.*' Marilyn Wright,
SCOTS INDEPENDENT

On the Trail of Robert Burns

John Cairney

ISBN 0 946487 51 0 PBK £7.99

Is there anything new to say about Robert Burns?

John Cairney says it's time to trash Burns the Brand and come on the trail of the real Robert Burns. He is the best of travelling companions on this convivial, entertaining journey to the heart of the Burns story.

Internationally known as 'the face of Robert Burns', John Cairney believes that the traditional Burns tourist trail urgently needs to find a new direction. In an acting career spanning forty years he has often lived and breathed Robert Burns on stage. *On the Trail of Robert Burns* shows just how well he can get under the skin of a character. This fascinating journey around Scotland is a rediscovery of Scotland's national bard as a flesh and blood genius.

On the Trail of Robert Burns outlines five tours, mainly in Scotland. Key sites include:

Alloway - Burns' birthplace. 'Tam O' Shanter' draws on the witch-stories about Alloway Kirk first heard by Burns in his childhood.

Mossgiel - between 1784 and 1786 in a phenomenal burst of creativity Burns wrote some of his most memorable poems including 'Holy Willie's Prayer' and 'To a Mouse.'

Kilmarnock - the famous Kilmarnock edition of *Poems Chiefly in the Scottish Dialect* published in 1786.

Edinburgh - fame and Clarinda (among others) embraced him.

Dumfries - Burns died at the age of 37. The trail ends at the Burns mausoleum in St Michael's churchyard.

'*For me an aim I never fash*
I rhyme for fun'.
ROBERT BURNS

'*My love affair on stage with Burns started in London in 1959. It was consumated on stage at the Traverse Theatre in Edinburgh in 1965 and has continued happily ever since*'.

JOHN CAIRNEY

'*The trail is expertly, touchingly and amusingly followed*'.
THE HERALD